THE 'BOYS ARE BACK

The Return of the Dallas Cowboys

★

Fort Worth Star-Telegram
The Summit Group

RODOLFO GONZALEZ

88

THE 'BOYS ARE BACK

The Return of the Dallas Cowboys

By Mike Fisher

and Richie Whitt

and The Staff
of the Fort Worth Star-Telegram

Fort Worth Star-Telegram
The Summit Group

Editors: Gary Hardee, Broc Sears
Photo Editor: Rodger Mallison
Cover Design: Greg Ice
Layout and Design: Rodger Mallison, Broc Sears
Copy Editor: Michael Towle
Desktop Editors: Marc Gilbert, Terisa Hart
Sports Editor: Mike Perry

Color Separations:
Barron Litho Plate Co. and Preston Barron
Fort Worth, Texas

PUBLISHED BY

Fort Worth Star-Telegram
400 West Seventh Street
Fort Worth, Texas 76102

The Summit Group
1227 West Magnolia
Suite 500
Fort Worth, Texas 76104

PUBLISHER'S CATALOGING IN PUBLICATION
(Prepared by Quality Books Inc.)

Fisher, Mike, 1959-
The 'Boys are back : the return of the Dallas Cowboys / Mike Fisher and Richie Whitt.
p. cm.
ISBN 1-56530-061-0

1. Dallas Cowboys (Football team)—History. 2. Super Bowl Game (Football). I. Whitt, Richie. II. Title. III. Title: The boys are back. IV. Title: The return of the Dallas Cowboys.

GV956.D3F47 1993 796.332 ' 64 ' 097642821
QB193-20120

MANUFACTURED IN THE UNITED STATES OF AMERICA
FIRST PRINTING, 1993

CONTENTS

FOREWORD

Back at the opening of training camp in July, I would have never believed that I'd be asked by my reporter friends at the *Fort Worth Star-Telegram* to write a foreword in a book covering the Dallas Cowboys' Super Bowl season. But here it is. Pinch me, please.

Only four years ago I was a struggling rookie quarterback on a 1-15 team going through the worst year of my life. Now I'm the Most Valuable Player for the Super Bowl champions. I went from a nightmare to a dream come true faster than anyone, including myself, ever thought was possible.

Experiencing our 1992 season was special, and it's something my teammates, our fans and I should be able to relive over and over again. From the grind of training camp, to the low of a last-second loss in Washington and finally to the high of Super Bowl Sunday in Pasadena, California, 1992 was a super season to savor. I hope you get as much enjoyment out of reliving these memories as we did creating them.

Troy Aikman
Quarterback
Dallas Cowboys

Jerry Hoefer

PAUL MOSELEY

ONE

Indelible Moments

Behind a security-guarded curtain, the showers of the Dallas Cowboys' dressing room in the bowels of the Rose Bowl are littered with damp towels and symbolism.

Beyond the curtain, hundreds of reporters crush each other in search of lustrous members of the just-crowned Super Bowl XXVII champions. They would love to locate Dave Wannstedt, the lame-duck defensive coordinator who is on his way to becoming the head coach of the Chicago Bears. And Michael Irvin, the mouthpiece of the team and centerpiece of the

★

SUPER BOWL XXVII
COWBOYS 52, BILLS 17

Troy Aikman has a Most Valuable Player day with four touchdown passes. The offense spreads around the scoring, made easier by a defense that forces nine turnovers. "We saved the best for last," Jimmy Johnson says.

★

"It is unbelievable. I am so filled with joy I can't even express it. If I could explode, I would. But I can't, because my insurance ain't paid up."

—Nate Newton
Cowboys Offensive Guard
January 31, 1993

passing game. And Golden Boy Troy Aikman, Super Bowl XXVII's Most Valuable Player after one of the most impressive quarterbacking days in the game's history.

But Wannstedt, Irvin and Aikman are almost by themselves in the shower area, creating symbols for the storylines they wrote during the Cowboys' amazing 1992 title run. Aikman cuts tape from his ankles, wadding it into balls and tossing them into a trash can with flawless accuracy. Irvin answers questions not with words but with charming facial expressions, then admires his contortions in the bathroom mirror. Wannstedt, naked and lathered up, runs across the slippery floor, trying not to fall.

"What were my numbers? I don't even know," asks Aikman. He is told: 22 of 30 for 273 yards, four touchdowns, no interceptions in the Super Bowl. The numbers parallel the dazzling statistics he piled up in the previous two playoff games, figures that, in terms of a single postseason, elevate him to all-time-great status.

"I gave the media my best stuff," boasts Irvin, who performs for post-game interviewers until almost 10 p.m., then parties so hard and long that by 6 a.m., when he is supposed to be ready for a flight to the Pro Bowl in Hawaii, he still hasn't returned to his hotel room.

"It's kinda sad it all has to end," mumbles Wannstedt, who will lose a longtime working association with close friend Jimmy Johnson, as well as his connection to the No. 1 defense that he helped build.

PAUL MOSELEY

MILTON ADAMS

Jimmie Jones plays a super game, returning one fumble two yards for a touchdown and recovering another to set up a Cowboys score. "I dreamed of that all week. Of course, I dreamed of making a little bit longer run," Jones says.

JOYCE MARSHALL

---★---

Troy Aikman drops to pass behind two Pro Bowl protectors, Mark Stepnoski and Nate Newton. "When the offensive line is protecting Troy the way they were today, it's no contest," says Jay Novacek.

---★---

Hindsight makes it all seems so logical. Millionaire oil-and-gas man buys the Dallas Cowboys in 1989. Hotshot college coach is hired. Can't-miss quarterback is combined with can't-miss receiver and can't-miss running back and can't-miss assistant coaches. A team that in 1989 was a talentless 1-15 now sees a roster bloated with silver-and-blue chippers who all play a hand in 1992's 13-3 regular season and dominating march through the playoffs. Many suggest that the Super Bowl XXVII champions are The Team of the '90s. The Super Bowl XXVII champions don't disagree.

"I've never shied away from the idea of a dynasty," Johnson says.

In a way, it is unfortunate that professional football is

RON JENKINS

such a what-have-you-done-lately business. Because when we look ahead so quickly, so many vignettes, so many snapshots, are left behind.

Many of the moments from the Cowboys' 52-17 dismantling of the Buffalo Bills are indelible. The defensive touchdowns from Jimmie Jones and Ken Norton, and the almost-touchdown by Leon Lett, who playfully, foolishly celebrates before crossing the goal line and loses the ball. Forced fumbles by Charles Haley. Irvin's grace in catching two touchdown passes. Emmitt Smith's inimitable stutter stepping. Tight end Jay Novacek's over-the-middle elusiveness. Alvin Harper's dunk over the crossbar. Four interceptions keyed by the play of a once-maligned secondary.

★

The Bills are ravaged for nine turnovers, four sacks and one lost quarterback. Ken Norton's hit in the second quarter knocks Buffalo quarterback Jim Kelly out of the game.

★

JERRY HOEFER

Milton Adams

Johnson celebrating at halftime with Dallas up 18 points, then receiving the team's official treatment near game's end when he is drenched with a bucket of ice, courtesy of guard Nate Newton, and his shellacked hair is mussed by Emmitt Smith.

But there are dozens of defining moments for the 1992 Dallas Cowboys, scenes behind curtains, behind sealed doors at Valley Ranch, behind the façades erected by public figures who, from an unwanted preseason game in Tokyo to a much-dreamed-of Super Bowl trip, had no concept of just how public they would become on January 31, 1993.

This is a collection of stories about those pivotal Cowboys. And some of those defining moments.

★

"The Cowboys haven't been on their backs all these years. They were just down on their knees."

Jerry Jones
Cowboys Owner
January 31, 1993

"Hoss, we're No. 1. We were as hot as smoke today."

Nate Newton
Cowboys Offensive Guard
January 31, 1993

Jerry Hoefer

Paul Moseley

Michael Irvin scores two touchdowns, but gives credit for the rout to the defense, including two goal-line stands. "Without that, we would have been in a pretty tough ballgame," he says. Ken Norton Jr. stops Bills running back Kenneth Davis for no gain on third down at the one-yard line in the first defensive stand.

Pages 20-21

On fourth down, Thomas Everett stops a Buffalo threat in the end zone with the first of his two interceptions. "We always knew what they were doing," he says.

PAUL MOSELEY

ARDNER
35
58
51
10

The Cowboys fall a few yards short of scoring the most points in Super Bowl history when Buffalo's Don Beebe knocks the ball out of Leon Lett's hand before he crosses the goal line. "I was running out of gas at about the 30," says Lett, who scooped up a fumble at the Cowboys' 38. "I was holding the ball out, trying to look sweet. I guess it backfired."

Jerry Hoefer

78

Ron Jenkins

Emmitt Smith rushes for 108 yards and one touchdown. "I think one of the greatest things that happened today was Emmitt rushing for over 100 yards," says teammate Michael Irvin. "It doesn't happen often against a team like the Bills, and once he got rolling, it was a big, big factor."

RON JENKINS

MILTON ADAMS

★

"If you don't stop the run, don't stop the play-action passes and don't pressure the quarterback, you're not going to be in the game."

SHANE CONLAN
BILLS LINEBACKER
JANUARY 31, 1993

★

TWO

Two Heads are Better than One

★

"There is no substitute for winning. I know it's an old cliché, but we must win. We will win."

JERRAL W. JONES
COWBOYS OWNER
FEBRUARY 25, 1989

★

To live, man requires air, water, food, shelter and sleep.

Jerry Jones and Jimmy Johnson require only air, water, food and shelter.

Jones and Johnson, the twin jet engines behind the light-speed ascent of the Dallas Cowboys to Super Bowl XXVII, don't follow the lead of former Philadelphia Eagles coach Dick Vermeil, who made tucking himself into a sleeping bag in his office fashionable. Jones and Johnson don't bunk next to their Valley Ranch desks. When there is work to be done and games to be won, they don't sleep at all.

Like on the day of the National Football Conference Championship Game January 17 in San Francisco. Unbeknownst to each other, the alarm clocks inside the heads of Jones and Johnson both sound at 4 a.m.

"I had some ideas I wanted to jot down that I thought would help us win," Johnson says.

"I had some things I wanted to map out for after we

Mark Gail

Joyce Marshall

Jimmy Johnson arrives at Dallas/Fort Worth Airport to succeed Tom Landry as coach of the Cowboys. Later, Jerry Jones and Johnson arrive at Cowboys headquarters.

MARK GAIL

★

"This is my life. I intend to invest a lot of my time, my hours, my life into this. ...I want an understanding of jocks and socks. ...[Every] decision will be mine."

Jerry Jones
Cowboys Owner
February 25, 1989

"It's tough when you break a relationship you've had for 29 years."

TEX SCHRAMM
FORMER COWBOYS
GENERAL MANAGER
FEBRUARY 25, 1989

★

won," Jones explains.

Johnson tells you that his carefully-coifed head hits the pillow at an hour that allows him only a vague concept of Jay Leno and no idea about David Letterman. If that's so, it's balanced by the fact that, as an early riser, he gets the worm. Or whatever else he strives for.

Since February of 1989, when the two former University of Arkansas football teammates arrived in the Metroplex — some say they squatted here only because Central Expressway and LBJ Freeway is where they fell off the turnip truck — they have pursued excellence relentlessly. Sometimes ruthlessly, too.

"I object to someone saying I'm running a cold busi-

ness here," Jones says. "I'm proud when I hear someone say I'm running a business, period."

Jones, 50, the always-grinnin', oil-and-gas man estimated to be worth three times the $140 million he paid to buy the franchise, has conducted his business and himself in a way that has pushed him toward the highest of National Football League ownership profiles. He has experienced fantastic success, not just running in the rat race, but buying the rights to it and then selling tickets and beer.

Johnson, 49, the always-calculating former University of Miami coach who turned a rookie 1-15 start in 1989 into a .500 record quicker than any man in National Football League history, is forever motivated

★

"He [Jones] has more enthusiasm than I believe any owner of the Cowboys has ever had. I think the Cowboys and the fans are in the best hands they could be placed in. ...He has the resources to do what the Cowboys need done."

Bum Bright
Former Cowboys Owner
February 25, 1989

★

MARK GAIL

"One of the greatest things to happen in the Cowboys' history is Jimmy Johnson joining the Dallas Cowboys. ...What Jimmy Johnson brings to the Cowboys will be worth more than five first-round draft picks or four Heisman Trophy winners."

Jerry Jones
Cowboys Owner
February 25, 1989

to travel on the fast track; he does not brake (or break) for children or small animals.

"I'm not saying other staffs don't work hard," Johnson says. "I know that anyone, to get to the National Football League, has to really put their noses to the grindstone. I'm just saying that from Jerry on down, no staff wants it more than we do. And no staff works harder than we do."

While Cowboys college scouting director Larry Lacewell is at the East-West Shrine Game in Palo Alto, California, in January, some uninitiated soul asks him to be specific about the names of the executives who run the Cowboys' various departments. Lacewell says "Jones" and "Johnson" are all anybody needs to know.

Ron Jenkins

Ron Jenkins

★

"There is no player that Jimmy Johnson feels greater about than Troy Aikman."

Jerry Jones
Cowboys Owner
February 25, 1989

★

RON JENKINS

Enthusiasm runs high for the new regime's first pre-season game in San Diego, but by the end of 1989, Jimmy Johnson endures a 1-15 nightmare.

"But an organization can't work that way," the outsider says.

"The hell it can't," Lacewell says. "We're in the Super Bowl, aren't we?"

The Cowboys' owner is also the general manager, the president of the Texas Stadium Corporation, the hands-on supervisor of almost every department in the organization and the head cheerleader (his lack of white boots notwithstanding). He literally wants to know how much his secretary, Marylyn Love, pays for pencils and coffee filters. He thinks of everything, right down to the silver-and-blue, chocolate-covered peanuts he offers visitors to his office.

The Cowboys' coach is the personnel director, the chief scout, the team psychologist and the emotional joystick of football's youngest team. He thinks of everything, too. One of the first changes he made was to remove the maze-like walls in the Valley Ranch locker room that had allowed cliques to form behind them. "Maybe some teams don't know how to make the moves that are necessary, or maybe they are too scared to make the moves," Johnson says.

Or maybe they're just sleeping in.

★

Jimmy Johnson, offensive coordinator Norv Turner and defensive coordinator Dave Wannstedt: The coaches "are like brothers," says Wannstedt's wife, Jan. "Sometimes Jimmy is the big brother. Sometimes Dave is his big brother."

★

Milton Adams

Milton Adams

Aaah, the dog days of summer, when Emmitt Smith dreams lazily of 2,000 yards, but won't speak of it.

MILTON ADAMS

1992 was a year when Troy Aikman would feel at home, both in training camp and with his head coach.

PAGES 36-37
Austin is Jimmy Johnson's kind of town, hot and humid, as offensive lineman Alan Veingrad knows.

Milton Adams

Jerry Hoefer

Jerry Hoefer

MILTON ADAMS

★

The Cowboys Shuffle: That's what John Gesek and the rest of the offensive line dance in training camp. Nate Newton moves from left tackle to right guard as offensive line coach Tony Wise juggles "a solid nucleus and veteran backups" to find a leakproof line.

★

THREE

Michael Irvin's Million-Dollar Toast

★

Emmitt Smith returns to his home state of Florida in the second preseason game and dazzles the home folks with some nifty runs and 63 yards.

Which is more demanding, Troy, the autograph seekers at training camp or the long airplane flight to Tokyo for an exhibition game?

★

No wonder wide receiver Michael Irvin and so many other unsigned veterans wondered during the 1992 training camp if Dallas Cowboys owner Jerry Jones would ever open his wallet.

Jones doesn't carry a wallet.

Check his front right-pants pocket. There is a money clip stuffed with domestic currency, featuring a foreign — to most of us — number of zeros. There is a credit card or two, and a driver's license. And there is Jones' crumpled, 2-inch-by-2-inch piece of paper.

"Everything I need to run the financial side of this organization is on this little piece of paper," says Jones, uncrumpling it to reveal a complex balance sheet with expenditures, revenues and profit margins.

Had Irvin and Dallas' other training-camp absentees had access to that crumpled little piece of paper, they might not have found themselves embroiled in a Summer of Discontent, during which nine players were involved in contract disputes. They might have

Paul Moseley

Milton Adams

Ron Jenkins

"We have reason to be concerned .... When we get back to Austin, it's back to the salt mines. And our guys had better pack a lunch, because there's going to be some long ones."

Dave Wannstedt
Defensive Coordinator
August 7, 1992

known sooner exactly how many dollars were available. Jones eventually found a crease in the little piece of paper that allowed Irvin, tight end Jay Novacek and center Mark Stepnoski to squeeze into uniform just before the season started. "Suddenly, we are business partners," said Irvin, who formed an odd alliance of sorts with Jones near midnight on September 3, 1992, when the two agreed on a three-year contract worth $1.25 million a season. Irvin became Jones' highest-paid player that night and immediately began sharing his new wealth with Jones, buying drinks for him as their champagne-soaked party moved from Jones' Valley Ranch office to the Cowboys Cafe, three blocks south.

ALLEN ROSE

Ron Jenkins

Their celebration would be repeated often during the 1992 season, and would be shared by other camp holdouts: like in the season-opening, 23-10 win over the Washington Redskins, when Irvin participated just four days after joining the club; or in Week 3, when Stepnoski reclaimed his starting position on the offensive line and helped the Cowboys to a 3-0 record when they plowed over the Phoenix Cardinals, 31-20; or in Week 11, when Novacek started a seven-game streak during which he caught six touchdown catches, including one in the 34-10 semifinal playoff win over the Philadelphia Eagles; and in the 30-20 NFC Championship Game victory over San Francisco,

★

Troy Aikman directs only one series in the last preseason game against Chicago, giving Steve Beuerlein playing time. In the regular season, Aikman stays healthy and Beuerlein stays on the sidelines.

★

Ron Jenkins

when two more summer holdouts, linebacker Ken Norton and safety James Washington, contributed key fourth-quarter interceptions.

"Look at all the guys who missed training camp, then had good seasons," Irvin says. "I ought to tell Jerry to ban training camp altogether."

Had Irvin done that, it still might not have topped his 1992 antics. It wasn't enough that he caught 78 passes for 1,396 yards. He also caught flak. For his new TV show. For missing the November 8 flight to Detroit. For involving himself in a melee over the late Jerome Brown, a friend who played for the Philadelphia Eagles before an automobile accident

★

While Bill Bates and Darren Woodson fight with the Bears, three Cowboy holdouts — Michael Irvin, Jay Novacek and Mark Stepnoski — watch.

★

Milton Adams

The Denver Broncos game offers few highlights for the offense while the defense gives fans a preview of the big plays it would make in the season ahead.

took his life. Eagles players called Irvin "disrespectful" of Brown's memory; Irvin thought the Eagles' use of Brown's old locker as a memorial was morbid.

But events like these never overshadow the celebrations staged by the ebullient Irvin. And like the figures atop a wedding cake, Irvin often finds himself joined by Jones in bliss. Their muddy hug after the NFC Championship Game, amidst the slop of rain-soaked Candlestick Park, was memorable not only for those who witnessed it, but for Jones' dry cleaner, who may never get the owner's best double-breasted gray suit back to normal.

Jones and Irvin competed against each other all summer. At September's Kickoff Luncheon at the Grand Kempinski Hotel in Addison, both men hoped they could seal the deal that would allow them to take the stage triumphantly. Instead, backstage contract talks broke off again for the millionth time. Jones ordered public-relations assistant Brett Daniels to the hotel lobby to ask Irvin to meet again. Irvin ordered Daniels to relay a nasty message back.

Hours and no agreement later, Jones was holed up in his office, feeling moved to privately repeat his belief that maybe Irvin was just a greedy nut. Irvin was outside his Carrollton home, picking up bricks scattered

★

Youngsters crowd by the field to watch their favorite players in the second preseason game against the Oilers.

★

ALLEN ROSE

"The last preseason game is always for the little people. It's a chance to either impress this team one last time or to make a good enough impression so that other teams take note of you."

DALE HELLESTRAE
COWBOYS BACKUP
OFFENSIVE LINEMAN
AUGUST 28, 1992

about his yard when lightning struck the house. He wondered if Jones wasn't a few bricks shy, too.

And it wasn't until daybreak on September 4, after Irvin had signed, that the two quit competing. Mere hours earlier, at the Cowboys Cafe, they had still been locked in battle.

"I'm buying this round!" Jones would bellow.

"Jerry, you just paid me a bunch of millions of dollars," Irvin would yell back. "I can afford to buy this round."

Ron Jenkins

Ron Jenkins

Game 1

Cowboys 23, Redskins 10. ABC-TV asks "Are You Ready For Some (Monday Night) Football?" The Redskins answer "We're not ready for the Cowboys," who block a punt for a safety on Washington's first possession and never trail.

Milton Adams

Milton Adams

JERRY HOEFER

Jimmie Jones starts at defensive tackle for an injured Tony Casillas and contributes two tackles and two assists. Alvin Harper steps around Darrell Green for a 26-yard touchdown, keeping the cheerleaders high stepping.

Jerry Hoefer

Game 2

Cowboys 34, Giants 28. Dallas builds 34–0 lead but barely hangs on via Michael Irvin's clock-killing catch.

"The big thing is we lost our intensity. When you play that well (early), you tend to lose a little bit."

Charles Haley
Cowboys Defensive End
September 13, 1992

Jerry Hoefer

With less than five minutes gone in the first quarter, Emmitt Smith dives over New York's defensive line and into the end zone.

Pages 54-55
Kelvin Martin takes a Troy Aikman pass 27 yards down the sideline.

Jerry Hoefer

47
47
25

2ND & 10
ON THE 41
SPORTS
AUTHORITY
FIRST
FIDELITY
103
52

PAUL MOSELEY

FOUR

Mutual Respect

It is November 18, 1990, at Anaheim Stadium. Two newspaper beat writers who cover the Dallas Cowboys watch every interaction between Cowboys quarterback Troy Aikman and coach Jimmy Johnson. As Aikman goes to Johnson on the sideline, the reporters' binoculars go to their eyes. As Johnson puts his arm on Aikman's shoulder, the writers put their elbows in each other's ribs.

The writers know Johnson supposedly has doubts about Aikman. They know Aikman definitely has doubts about Johnson. And they know that before this game against the Los Angeles Rams, Aikman had seriously contemplated banging on Johnson's hotel suite door with a "trade me" demand.

All of this makes Johnson's gesture look ridiculously forced.

Now it is January 14, 1993, and Aikman and Johnson have another problem. Another conflict born of dis-

★

GAME 3

Cowboys 31, Cardinals 20. Michael Irvin catches an 87-yard touchdown pass on Dallas' first series. Jay Novacek had three catches for 28 yards as the two training camp holdouts started to exert their influence on the offense.

★

JERRY HOEFER

	Rec.	Yds.	Lg.	TD
IRVIN	8	210	87	3

Jerry Hoefer

"I don't want to hear another thing about rust or holdout. That's in the past. In fact, after today, I don't want to hear anything about this game."

Michael Irvin
Cowboys Wide Receiver
September 20, 1993

PAUL MOSELEY

Ken Norton and Larry Brown join forces in recovering a Phoenix fumble.

trust? Another battle between stubborn egos? Another trade demand? Hardly. Aikman and Johnson agree they need to talk about what they're going to do about those Cowboys players angry because they don't have access to more playoff tickets.

"Maybe we need to go to Jerry Jones and explain the situation," Aikman tells Johnson, who does just that.

"Maybe we need to get with some of the players and make them understand we have no control over some of this," Johnson tells Aikman, who does just that.

Aikman says he and Johnson talked more in the closing weeks of the 1992 season than they had talked in some entire years before that. Not all game-plan stuff, either. Mexican food. Country music. The kind of things two people who've worked together for four years — people who absolutely need each other no matter how unwilling they had once been to admit it — talk about.

Before the Cowboys' 34-10 playoff victory over Philadelphia, Aikman phones a reporter to discuss a *Fort Worth Star-Telegram* story about the relationship between the quarterback and the coach. In it Johnson said he needed Aikman because "he's the type of quarterback who fits my personality perfectly." Johnson also said the two once had "a strained rela-

★

Outstanding performances by the secondary are upstaged by Phoenix's 383 passing yards.

★

JERRY HOEFER

★

GAME 4

Eagles 31, Cowboys 7. Four turnovers and a season-high 160 rushing yards against Dallas' defense spell the Cowboys' demise in a much-ballyhooed Monday night showdown before a huge television audience and a frenzied Philadelphia crowd.

★

tionship'' and "we had our differences."

"That's the first time he's ever admitted we had some problems," Aikman says. "And that other stuff, that's some of the nicest things he's ever said about me."

Neither Johnson nor Aikman are insecure men. Johnson says, "I might have once had some insecurities, years ago, but I have no room for that now." Of Aikman, family friend and Aikman Enterprises director Verna Riddles says, "People have apparently mistaken Troy's humility for insecurity. Because believe me, he's about the most confident, secure person I've ever met."

But in the four years since Johnson arrived as the big-name college coach and Aikman, the 1989 first-round pick, arrived as the big-name college player, they have come to a realization. There is a hole in Aikman that Johnson fills. And Aikman plugs a Johnson gap, too.

The meshing was a factor in 1992, Aikman's breakout year. Aikman finished the 16-game regular season with career bests in passing yards (3,445), touchdown passes (23) and quarterback rating (89.5, the second-highest figure among full-time NFL quarterbacks). He beat Redskins, Chiefs, Raiders, Broncos, Eagles and critics who wailed that he couldn't throw deep or think deep. On November 15, Aikman failed to con-

Ron Jenkins

Ron Jenkins

Ron Jenkins

nect on what would have been a game-winning scoring pass in a 27-23 loss to the Los Angeles Rams. "He'll never be Roger Staubach," they said. On December 6, Aikman led Dallas on a classic late drive to beat the Denver Broncos. "Oh, Roger did that lots of times," they said.

Now it is January 17, 1993. Johnson is about to conclude a post-NFC Championship Game news conference when he spots Aikman waiting to take a turn at the mike. Aikman had just given the performance of his life: 24 of 34, 322 yards, two touchdowns, no interceptions. Johnson says, "Troy's come a long way, and he's brought me with him." Then Johnson climbs off the stage.

Just as Johnson reaches to put his arms around Aikman's shoulders, two beat writers who cover the Cowboys jab each other in the ribs. It strikes them that Johnson's gesture does not look forced. It does not look ridiculous. It looks sincere. And touching. And as significant as anything that happened in the Dallas Cowboys' 1992 championship season.

★

Veterans Stadium — a very lonely place.

"You can't expect us to win making the mistakes we did out there."

JIMMY JOHNSON
HEAD COACH
OCTOBER 5, 1992

★

PAUL MOSELEY

PAUL MOSELEY

PAUL MOSELEY

GAME 5

Cowboys 27, Seahawks 0. The defense allows a franchise-record low of 62 yards. Rookie linebacker Robert Jones did his part, at one point snuffing Seattle's only scoring threat with a sack that puts Seahawks quarterback Dan McGwire out of the game with a separated shoulder. The only down note for the Cowboys is the loss of Bill Bates, who suffers a torn ligament in his knee. "That was the lowest point," Bates says. "From there, it was either go into deep depression or accept the situation and make the most of it."

★

GAME 6

Cowboys 17, Chiefs 10. Ray Horton's interception inside Dallas' 20–yard line in the last two minutes seals it. The victory puts Dallas alone in first place in the NFC for the first time since Week 15 of 1985. But the Chiefs make the Cowboys work for it. Emmitt Smith carries his share of the load for a 95-yard day.

★

RON JENKINS

22

Allen Rose

Defensive lineman Jim Jeffcoat drapes Kansas City quarterback Dave Krieg, who manages only 16 completions in 31 attempts. The Cowboys' other line, anchored by center Mark Stepnoski, limits the Chiefs' bookend pass rushers, Neil Smith and Derrick Thomas, to one sack.

Allen Rose

JOYCE MARSHALL

PAUL MOSELEY

FIVE

Enigmatic Emmitt Smith

As the roaming herd of minicams, microphones and notepads stampedes toward Emmitt Smith's locker, the Dallas Cowboys running back drops his head and rolls his eyes. Before the first question spews forth, Smith reminds the pack he is fond of brevity. Remember, he doesn't really like all this attention.

Whoosh. Consider that a spin move complete with a stiff-arm, courtesy of the National Football League's two-time rushing champion.

Four days before the team's opening playoff game against the Philadelphia Eagles, Smith fuels the enigma. At a Dallas Mavericks game, he gladly signs autographs, high-fives fans, poses for the Reunion Arena scoreboard video and volunteers to help spice up a halftime show featuring children's bowling.

Remember, he doesn't really like all this attention.

"I like dealing with the media and I like the fans," Smith says. "It's when they cross that line that we

---

GAME 7

Cowboys 28, Raiders 13. Emmitt Smith rushes for 152 yards and three touchdowns before a crowd of more than 90,000 in Los Angeles. Smith takes a blow in the back that sends him to the sidelines but doesn't stop him. "I was ready to let him sit awhile," Jimmy Johnson says. "But he says, 'Coach, I got to go back in.' If he's ready to go, I'm ready to go with him."

A trophy: Backup Leon Lett gets into the game in the second quarter and recovers a fumble. "Everybody's playing and everybody's happy," Lett says.

have problems. That turns me off."

Smith the personality is as difficult to dissect as Smith the runner is to tackle. In both arenas he dodges, darts, spins, slashes and befuddles. He can seem sincerely shy one minute, rude the next. Ten minutes later, he can flip-flop those faces, or put on his "gamer," the serious face where his mouth and mind open without prying and his personality sparkles as brightly as his diamond earrings, gold necklaces and wide, attentive eyes. Call it the limp-leg approach to media relations. To meet Emmitt Smith is to be an opposing defender: You're not sure what Smith is allowing you to grab or how long he'll let you hold on.

Shortly after a May minicamp workout, Smith stares into an interviewer's notebook and speaks emotionally, almost reverently, about wanting to rush for 2,000 yards. Once said, he spends the remainder of the season joking about the subject and brushes away related questions with the same determination he uses when wiping water spots off his precious burgundy Mercedes convertible.

In October, he shouts about wanting to renegotiate his contract and "be paid among the best." A month later, he rejects a $5.76 million extension, which would have put his salary in the same neighborhood as Detroit Lions back Barry Sanders' contract. Smith says he "wanted to set new standards."

When ESPN poses a contract question after the December 21 Monday night game in Atlanta, Smith

PAUL MOSELEY

It is Emmitt's day in L.A., but Daryl Johnston, Smith's straight man, gets to carry the ball. Once.

RODGER MALLISON

RODGER MALLISON

Emmitt is doing it, so Troy Aikman does it, too. He runs a bootleg for a three–yard touchdown, diving over the goal line for emphasis. "Twenty of 21 times we run that play, I end up throwing it," Aikman says. "I didn't feel particularly fast, but I got in".

RODGER MALLISON

Jerry Jones chats with defensive tackle Russell Maryland as the game winds down. The emotion in Dallas' locker room afterward says this isn't just another victory.

puts his hand over the microphone, spits out a chuckle and prances away from the live interview.

So which side is the real Smith? All of them. He's the passionate, caring teammate who announces to no one that he gave his Eagles' game ball to injured veteran Bill Bates. He's the superstar who showcases each of his touchdown balls in a trophy case. He's the selfish boy who wants more money, the youngster who changed his given name of Emmit to Emmitt, thinking the extra "T" would separate him from his father and grandfather, who both have the same name.

He's the generous man who thanks his offensive linemen with round-trip airline tickets. He bought the

GAME 8

Cowboys 20, Eagles 10. Emmitt Smith stuns Philadelphia with 163 rushing yards and Dallas' defense begins its number-one reign. Dallas moves to 7–1, and the Eagles fall to 5–3.

JOSE JAUREZ

Paul Moseley

land and the houses in Pensacola, Florida, where three generations of Smiths now live. He's single and sometimes lonely. But he's also a playboy bachelor who goes to watch dancers at a Dallas topless bar after home victories. He's the guy who detests posing for photographs. And he's the guy financing a successful sports memorabilia business in Florida called Emmitt, Inc.

The other cog in Dallas' rushing machine is easier to evaluate. With the offensive line of tackles Mark Tuinei and Erik Williams, guard Nate Newton and John Gesek, and center Mark Stepnoski, what you see is what you get. In 1992, what you didn't see was traps, sweeps or tricks. It is a unit that overcame and eventu-

★

What's a Dallas–Philadelphia game without controversy? Did Herschel Walker score by holding the ball over the goal line? One referee says yes, another says Walker fumbled. A third rules neither, giving the ball back to the Eagles.

★

In the third quarter, with the Eagles leading 7–3, Kelvin Martin comes through with two critical catches, one to keep the drive alive, followed by a 22–yard touchdown.

Paul Moseley

Ron Jenkins

ally benefitted from a training camp shuffle to open holes for Smith (1,713 rushing yards), keep quarterback Troy Aikman healthy (only 23 sacks) and break out of anonymity (Williams earned Player of-the-Week honors in November, and Stepnoski and Newton were Pro Bowlers).

★

Games against the Eagles are always head–butting contests. Even the fans come prepared.

★

But no doubt Smith is the focus, fuzzy as it is. You want clarity? You get it only when Emmitt wants to give it. He's the guy who shrugs off the importance of the NFC Championship Game during a noon press conference on January 14, then hours later dances and high-steps 69,700 fans into a frenzy at a Texas Stadium pep rally. Remember, Smith doesn't really like all this attention.

MILTON ADAMS

★

GAME 9

Cowboys 37, Lions 3. Russell Maryland recovers a loose ball as the Cowboys get revenge for the previous season's playoff loss to the Lions.

★

MILTON ADAMS

Kenny Gant adjusts Mel Gray's head. "The word 'revenge' never was actually said," Dave Wannstedt says after his defense shuts down the Lions.

Milton Adams

★

Game 10

Rams 27, Cowboys 23. Quarterback Troy Aikman's pass to Kelvin Martin in the end zone falls incomplete on the game's final play of the shocking upset. "This was a good lesson for us, I hope," says Jim Jeffcoat.

★

Ron Jenkins

Jerry Hoefer

Jerry Hoefer

88

51

5
30

Ron Jenkins

55

Ron Jenkins

Game 11

Cowboys 16, Cardinals 10. Even without injured defensive end Charles Haley, the defense shuts down Phoenix in an ugly game. Alvin Harper's third–quarter touchdown gives Dallas the winning edge.

RODOLFO GONZALEZ

GAME 12

Cowboys 30, Giants 3. Emmitt Smith scores on a 60-yard run and New York rookie quarterback Kent Graham is overmatched by Dallas' defense. The victory is a sweet dessert for fans full of turkey.

JOSE JUAREZ

"It wasn't pretty, and maybe our offense is that way because we know teams aren't going to score many. But if you would have predicted we'd have 10 wins after 12 games, we would have taken it."

TROY AIKMAN
COWBOYS QUARTERBACK
NOVEMBER 26, 1992

Jose Juarez

★

The victory was Dallas' first season sweep of the Giants since 1987. The defense holds New York to three downs on six of their 13 possessions. "It was a hard way to break into pro football," says Giants rookie quarterback Kent Graham.

★

Jose Juarez

Jose Juarez

The victory brings smiles to some faces, but not Jimmy Johnson's. "We need to be sharper. I don't want us below a level I expect," he says afterwards.

Milton Adams

SIX

Evolution of a Defense

A banana hangs by a piece of athletic tape in Charles Haley's locker, put there by some of his Cowboys teammates. They are amused by Haley's comfortable acceptance of a public image as a schizoid Neanderthal, one that would befuddle Charles Darwin. It is their way of needling him back after he takes another acidic shot. "Hey Charles, why don't you go in the corner somewhere and evolve," they say.

After six years, three Pro Bowls and countless "incidents" (such as urinating on teammate Tim Harris' car, punching walls, telling San Francisco Coach George Seifert where to stick his head), the San Francisco 49ers, Haley's first team in 1992, tired of the 6-foot-5, 240-pound defensive lineman's antisocial antics. Alcatraz was closer, but it's closed. So the 49ers shipped Haley to the Cowboys, who are to trade-hungry NFL teams what 7-Eleven is to starving insomniacs: open 24 hours.

Haley's contributions to the Cowboys were debated

Allen Rose

★

Game 13

Cowboys 31, Broncos 27. Troy Aikman engineers an 80-yard drive in the final five minutes, capping a wild game in which the quarterback-shuttling Broncos score two touchdowns on trick plays.

★

almost daily on radio talk shows throughout the 1992 season. He had more profane exchanges with reporters than sacks (six), and his 39 tackles ranked him 12th on the team. But even Tony Tolbert, the other defensive end whose work was unfairly ignored by Haley chroniclers, concedes that Haley "gave us that intangible thing. He'd been to two Super Bowls. He had a presence. Our offense already had Troy Aikman and Emmitt Smith and Michael Irvin and those guys. But Charles gave our defense its first impact player."

Haley's impact was felt when he didn't play. Nursing a groin injury, he didn't make the trip to Phoenix for the November 22 game against the Cardinals. When Dallas won, 16-10, virtually every member of the defense crowed, "We're no one-man team."

Of course, the Cowboys defense was more like a 21-man team. Seven linemen (starters Haley, Tolbert, Russell Maryland and Tony Casillas; reserves Jimmie Jones, Leon Lett and sack leader Jim Jeffcoat) rolled in and out in situations. Top tackler Ken Norton led a five-pack of linebackers that included Robert Jones, Vinson Smith, Godfrey Myles and Dixon Edwards. And almost constant tinkering with the defensive backfield milked it of contributions from nine men: "Cradle Corners" Kevin Smith and Larry Brown, at 21 and 22, respectively, the NFL's youngest cornerback combo; safeties Thomas Everett, James Washington and Ray Horton, who complained the rotation system

ALLEN ROSE

Charles Haley takes and receives a "hands on" approach during the Denver game.

PAGES 100–101:
A jubilant Michael Irvin and Issiac Holt head out of Mile High Stadium and into a berth in the NFC playoffs.

ALLEN ROSE

ALLEN ROSE

NFL

RODGER MALLISON

RODGER MALLISON

made him feel "like a leper"; and subs Darren Woodson, Bill Bates, Issiac Holt and Kenny Gant, who swiped the idea of the "Shark" dance from teammate Kevin Smith and became a sensation.

Was it a dominant defense? The numbers say so. Dallas permitted just 15 points per game, led the NFL in preventing third-down conversions, allowed more than 100 rushing yards in a game just three times and more than 300 passing yards in a game just twice, and doubled its sack total of the previous year. Still none of them made the Pro Bowl, joining the 1983 Cincinnati Bengals as the only teams to be No. 1 in defense and have zero representatives in the all-star game in

★

GAME 14

Redskins 20, Cowboys 17. Dallas' collapse includes Troy Aikman's goal-line interception, Michael Irvin's fumble and Emmitt Smith's underhanded throw out of the end zone, which results in Washington's winning touchdown.

★

RODGER MALLISON

"We -- it away. That's very uncharacteristic for us. We played our butts off, but at the end the breaks went to the other team. Stuff happens."

John Gesek
Cowboys Offensive Lineman
December 13, 1992

Hawaii. And while some members of the defense used the snub as a rallying point, Cowboys insiders acknowledge that the Dallas defense sent exactly the right number of players to the Pro Bowl. "We've got so many guys whose contributions have been about equal that maybe we really don't have those one or two guys who stand out," says defensive coordinator Dave Wannstedt.

But eventually, credit came. A Super Bowl tends to do for the anonymous what even a 13-3 regular-season record, an NFC East title and an NFC Championship Game appearance cannot.

"We're getting famous for not being famous," Norton says.

RODGER MALLISON

"And to think, we pride ourselves on efficiency."

MICHAEL IRVIN
COWBOYS WIDE RECEIVER
DECEMBER 13, 1992

SEVEN

The Glass is Half Full

GAME 15

Cowboys 41, Falcons 17. Emmitt Smith rushes for a season-high 174 yards as Dallas cruises on Monday Night Football.

It is October 25, 1992, and for one of the first times in ten years, Bill Bates watches a Dallas Cowboys game instead of playing in one. His surgically-repaired left knee rests in a recliner in his north Dallas living room. He watches almost in a state of shock as teammates take the Los Angeles Coliseum field to play the Raiders without him. Shock shifts into uneasiness, then deteriorates into nausea. It is almost a test of faith. Bill Bates, a card-carrying member of the Fellowship of Christian Athletes devoted to (in order) God, family and Cowboys, needs a beer.

"I was going crazy. I was mad, sad and I couldn't watch anymore," says Bates, who realizes that no amount of beer will change the facts. His knee still hurts, his season is still over, and his Cowboys prove what, in the back of Bates' mind, he almost hoped was impossible — they can win without him.

"I felt lonely," he says. "I felt like a piece of me was missing. My conscience knew I should be there but my

CAROLYN BAUMAN

Carolyn Bauman

★

The sweeping curve of Atlanta's new Georgia Dome frames receiver Kelvin Martin's second-quarter TD celebration.

★

Carolyn Bauman

★

The Dallas Cowboys set three goals for the 1992-93 season:

No. 1, make the playoffs.

No. 2, win the NFC East.

No. 3, go to the Super Bowl.

After the Atlanta game they know two out of three is not good enough.

★

GAME 16

Cowboys 27, Bears 14. Emmitt Smith wins the rushing title, and the defense wins the No. 1 crown by holding Chicago to 92 yards in Mike Ditka's, Mike Singletary's and Curvin Richards' final game.

Russell Maryland picks off a deflected toss and chugs 26 yards into the end zone. Maryland's celebration is emphatic if not artistic.
"I told Russell, 'If you're going to do a belly-flop, at least wait until you're in a pool.' I've never seen anyone do a flop on Astroturf."

TONY CASILLAS
COWBOYS DEFENSIVE LINEMAN
DECEMBER 27, 1992

JOSE JUAREZ

body wouldn't let me. That was the lowest point. From there, it was either go into deep depression or accept the situation and make the most of it."

For eye-opening reasons off the field, Bates will fondly recall 1992. He'll also always fight the temptation to think, "What if?" On a routine kickoff coverage against the Seattle Seahawks on October 11, Bates' foot caught awkwardly in the Texas Stadium turf, tearing three knee ligaments.

"I went through mental denial," Bates says. "I was telling doctors who had seen a thousand knees that they were crazy. I went looking for any quack to tell me I could play."

Not only was Bates' season over, his financial gam-

Carolyn Bauman

Paul Moseley

ble also backfired. Shortly before training camp in July, Bates, the kamikaze long shot who had hung on for ten seasons thanks more to tenacity than talent, passed on a $350,000 contract offer and signed a one-year, split deal that paid him a base salary of $200,000 and another $250,000 if he stayed on the active roster. But on October 12, Bates was no longer active. His placement on permanent injured reserve cost him $171, 875.

Despite being forced to observe a season he had always dreamed of taking part in, Bill Bates reinvented himself and found a way to contribute. "I became the team's biggest cheerleader," he says.

Before the team's January 10 playoff game against

the Philadelphia Eagles, Bates gave his McKinney ranch to the Cowboys fans, opening the place up for a free pep rally attended by close to 20,000 on a rainy, cold Friday night. "It was unbelievable," Bates says. "We had to call out 15 sheriffs just to keep things under control, but it was great. I went outside and I felt like a rock star. Then as I sat looking out a window in the ranch house, all I could see for miles in both directions were headlights. It tingled my spine. It was like a *Field of Dreams*."

That celebration set the stage for a Texas Stadium gathering the next week, at which 69, 700 Cowboys followers gave the club a send-off before the NFC title game in San Francisco.

Dallas Cowboys fans rallied. And in what he realized could be his first and last Super Bowl, Bill Bates rallied, too.

★

With a playoff appearance dead ahead, the tide of Cowboys T-shirts, caps and frenzied fans begins to surge. The first wave would hit Philadelphia.

★

RODGER MALLISON

DIVISIONAL PLAYOFF

Cowboys 34, Eagles 10. Troy Aikman maintains his "just-like-any-other-game" attitude up until kickoff. Emmitt Smith runs for 114 yards, Aikman throws for 200, and Dallas holds onto the ball for 35 minutes. The defense shuts down the Eagles' running game and sacks Randall Cunningham for 45 yards in losses. Dallas' big D keeps getting better.

RODGER MALLISON

Jerry Hoefer

JERRY HOEFER

92
92
21
21

EIGHT

Night of the Living Play

★

"We may not have any (defensive) players going to the Pro Bowl, but that's OK. We don't need any individual stars; we've got a team, and that's what defense is, a team effort."

RUSSELL MARYLAND
COWBOYS DEFENSIVE TACKLE
JANUARY 10, 1993

"If you don't believe we are the most physical defense in the league, go ask the Eagles what they think."

JIM JEFFCOAT
COWBOYS DEFENSIVE END
JANUARY 10, 1993

★

Dallas Cowboys center Mark Stepnoski didn't see any of it coming. Not the blind-side collision with Washington Redskins linebacker Wilber Marshall, not the Cowboys' improbable collapse at RFK Stadium, and certainly not the flight home to Dallas/Fort Worth Airport — including an unscheduled stop in Hell — that followed Dallas' come-from-ahead-loss in Washington on December 13, 1992.

With Dallas leading, 17-13, midway through the final quarter, receiver Michael Irvin latches on to a Troy Aikman rifle shot and heads upfield. But when cornerback Darrell Green strips the ball away from Irvin, the Cowboys lose their composure. On Danny Copeland's return of the fumble, Marshall puts Stepnoski on his butt. On the Redskins' ensuing possession, the Dallas defense mounts a four-down, goal-line stand. And Stepnoski fights to control the thoughts racing fuzzily through his mind.

"I'm hurt," Stepnoski admits to himself, struggling

Ron Jenkins

Troy Aikman congratulates center Mark Stepnoski after Derrick Gainer scores their last touchdown of the game.

"I'm probably the biggest idiot in this room, but I didn't really feel like we had the game won until we scored the last touchdown."

Troy Aikman
Cowboys Quarterback
January 10, 1993

Jerry Hoefer

Ken Norton Jr. knocks the ball loose from Eagles running back Herschel Walker, then makes the recovery. Pumped up and proud, he makes his point to the Texas Stadium crowd.

to master the sting of a right hip pointer. "But this is the Redskins, RFK Stadium, the fourth quarter." And he limps back onto the field for a key offensive series that would start inside Dallas' 3-yard line.

"Looking back, I shouldn't have been in the game," Stepnoski says. "But I didn't want to make excuses then and I won't now."

On the second play of the possession, Stepnoski cannot firmly plant his leg for leverage. He is pushed back into Aikman's face by an indistinct Redskins lineman named Jason Buck. A surprised Aikman tries to stop his throwing motion but loses the ball as he is tackled. Running back Emmitt Smith picks up the ball, and in a monumentally bone-headed play, tries to sling it as he

Jerry Hoefer

Jerry Hoefer

RON JENKINS

Troy Aikman slowly gains confidence as the game progresses. By the end of the game, he has completed 12 of his last 15 passes. There are no fumbles and no interceptions.

is tackled. After a wild end-zone scramble, the Redskins recover, and the Cowboys wind up with one of what would be only three losses in 16 regular-season games.

Coach Jimmy Johnson, who moaned about "too many functions" during his team's preseason trip to Tokyo, despises traveling. For Johnson, traveling after losing is a frightening equation. As the team and media board the charter, Johnson takes his familiar front-row, left-side seat beside defensive coordinator Dave Wannstedt and begins his ritual: watching a game tape with headphones on. But he doesn't sit comfortably for long.

Dallas broadcaster Dale Hansen watches as backup

Jerry Hoefer

center Frank Cornish, rookie middle linebacker Robert Jones and finally, even offensive coordinator Norv Turner, hear and feel Johnson's wrath.

"It was far from a party plane," says Hansen, the WFAA-TV sports anchor and KVIL-FM commentator who sat to the right behind Johnson. "But when Jimmy got up, you could tell it was trouble. He told Frank to wipe the grin off his face and then he screamed at Robert to sit down. Then he told Norv to find a seat. Jimmy crossed the line. By the time we landed, players were madder about the flight than losing the game."

Says Dallas' long-time radio play-by-play voice Brad Sham: "The mood at the start of the flight was nothing different than usual. Then Jimmy jumped on Frank

★

shark (shärk) **n.** [prob. < G. *schurke,* scoundrel, rogue] **1.** a person who victimizes others **2.** (slang) a person with great ability in a given activity. **3.** an aggressive and fierce marine animal. **4.** a celebration dance performed by Kenny Gant.

★

Joyce Marshall

Almost 70,000 fans pack into Texas Stadium for a pep rally; hollering, waving banners and towels, and cheering their heroes.

"At first I didn't want to come, but when I came out earlier for interviews, I got goose bumps."

Mike Saxon
Cowboys Punter
January 14, 1993

and Robert. He told them to 'sit their ass down', even though in Jones' case someone else was in his seat playing cards. After Jimmy pulled that, the guys were seething."

The confrontations, however, aren't over. First, Hansen watches Johnson cancel after-dinner drinks and dessert. "We had nothing but orange juice from Kentucky on," Hansen says. By then, an hour into the flight, Johnson's temper tantrum has the plane looking and sounding like a morgue. Nobody moves. Nobody talks. Suddenly, Hansen feels the cabin get even quieter, colder. As he kneels over his seat and plays blackjack with Spanish radio producer Israel Aguilar, Hansen senses an imposing figure at his side.

"I could hear Jimmy breathing and I sensed his lips

Joyce Marshall

Joyce Marshall

Paul Mosley

Paul Mosley

pursing like they do when he's about to pop," Hansen says. "I sat there for what seemed like an hour wondering if I should stand up to him or back down and lose the respect of the players."

Hansen later asked offensive line coach Tony Wise what he would've done.

"He told me he would have jumped," Hansen says. "He said the chances of falling from 35,000 feet were better than what I did."

But Hansen is calm in the eye of Johnson's storm.

"Finally, I looked him in the eye and said, 'Coach, how are you doing?' Then I turned to Israel, who couldn't deal because he was shaking so bad, and said, 'Hit me.' Jimmy left and we've never talked about it."

★

NFC Championship Game

Cowboys 30, 49ers 20. Jimmy Johnson comes to Candlestick Park for a first-hand inspection of the soggy field. Approximately 28,000 square feet of new sod is laid before kickoff.

★

Jerry Hoefer

★

Troy Aikman sets a team playoff completion record and throws for a season-high 322 yards. "Troy's come a long way, and he's brought me with him," says Jimmy Johnson. Dallas dominates after a 10-10 halftime tie. Kevin Smith has seven tackles. Tony Casillas records three sacks.

★

Milton Adams

MILTON ADAMS

JERRY HOEFER

★

Oh, Emmitt, what a day! Running for 114 yards. Catching passes for 59 yards. Scoring two touchdowns. Kelvin Martin's game-clinching touchdown reception isn't as sensational as "The Catch" of 1982, but his teammates are more than happy with the result.

★

67
28

CAROLYN BAUMAN

"We haven't gotten any credit all year, and I don't suppose we're going to get any right now. But we've been doing some good things against good people all year."

VINSON SMITH
COWBOYS LINEBACKER
JANUARY 17, 1993

Carolyn Bauman

NINE

Coaches on the Border

★

Daryl Johnston rarely has remarkable statistics, but he often makes big plays. On special teams, he grabs a 49ers fumble in midair to set up Dallas' first field goal.

★

One hand tilts the glass of Heineken on ice, the other steers a tortilla chip into a bowl of On The Border salsa. It's Friday night at a Dallas restaurant. And if you didn't know just how difficult the Dallas Cowboys coach can be to live with — "I'm a control freak," he freely admits — you would wonder why one of the most popular men in town seems so alone.

Then Jimmy Johnson's friends filter in.

Through the front door marches offensive line coach Tony Wise, joined by his cigar. Next comes Nick Christin, Johnson's lawyer and pal. Here comes Cowboys public-relations man Rich Dalrymple and his wife, Roz. Then special-teams coach Joe Avezzano and wife, Diann. Finally defensive coordinator Dave Wannstedt and his wife, Jan.

These visits to the Mexican restaurant take place every Friday night. And if an outsider doesn't realize by now that Johnson has as many friends as he needs and is friendlier to what he calls "gang" than you

Jerry Hoefer

"I got so sick of seeing 'The Catch.' Now maybe they will show mine just as much. We kicked butt and hopefully we also erased some memories."

Alvin Harper
Cowboys Wide Receiver
January 17, 1993

might think, Jan Wannstedt is more than willing to set you straight.

"They are all like brothers," she says. "Sometimes, Jimmy is the big brother. Sometimes, Dave is his big brother. When you get inside the group, you see what sort of a person Jimmy really is, and what sort of relationships he's truly capable of. I mean, you should see him with our daughters (Keri and Jami). They really love him."

So does their dad. Which made Dave Wannstedt's post-Super Bowl move to the head coaching job with the Chicago Bears a bittersweet switch. Wannstedt has been Johnson's protégé for 15 years, except for brief departures to work at the University of Southern

Jerry Hoefer

California and with the Miami Dolphins. They were together at the University of Pittsburgh, at Oklahoma State, at the University of Miami, and now for four years in Dallas. By 1992, 40-year-old Dave Wannstedt had developed and sharpened a knack for playing off Johnson, for knowing when to be a "yes man," when to be a "yes, but" man, and when to strongly suggest Johnson put a lid on it.

Seconds after Alvin Harper's 70-yard reception, which set up the game-clinching score, a rainbow appears over Candlestick. "God was looking down on his team," Emmitt Smith says.

In 1992, Wannstedt had a role. In Jimmy's universe, who doesn't? Defensive line coach Butch Davis' fiery, overzealous, attack-dog style angers many players on offense, but, by Johnson's design, they are *supposed* to be incited by it. Running backs coach Joe Brodsky is more of an avuncular stand-up comic than he is Xs-

★

Erik Williams plays so hard he winds up dehydrated and slumped over a canister in the locker room while his teammates celebrate the victory.

★

and-Os man. But Johnson saw long ago that Brodsky's persona is far from a weakness; it's a mood-dictating strength. Some Dallas assistants, such as Steve Hoffman, Robert Ford, Bob Slowik and Davis, burn with ambition. Others, such as receivers coach Hubbard Alexander, secondary coach Dave Campo, Wise and Avezzano, have the skills to climb the occupational ladder. But all they burn is the candle. At both ends.

"It is a very tight group," says second-year offensive coordinator Norv Turner, a relative newcomer among the key staffers. "There has to be a certain fit to a coaching staff. With Jimmy, nothing is happenstance."

Wannstedt's departure to a head coaching job certainly isn't. Bob Fosse never choreographed moves like this one.

Johnson pushed hard in January 1992 for Wannstedt to get the Pittsburgh Steelers head coaching position. Wannstedt, who meticulously planned the return to his hometown on the assumption that his resumé and Johnson's influence would be enough, was crushed when another Pittsburgh native, Bill Cowher, won the job. Steelers president Dan Rooney was said to be taken back by Wannstedt's forceful sense of purpose. During one meeting, Wannstedt unloaded a briefcase full of detailed plans that covered everything from how much he wanted his assistants to be paid to what sort of players he would select in the upcoming college draft. "Maybe I came on too strong," Wannstedt

Jerry Hoefer

says.

But in December 1992, when the University of Pittsburgh called, Wannstedt came on strong again. Pitt's "money men" wanted Wannstedt to return to his alma mater and be their coach. They had the authority to offer him the job. They went through Johnson, who in effect acted as his friend's agent. The money men said how about a five-year, guaranteed contract worth $1.5 million. Wannstedt told Johnson to tell them how about ten years, but told himself he would settle for six.

Jerry Jones prowls the sideline in his silk suit and galoshes. "That wasn't too becoming," he says. Your're entitled to it, Jerry.

The wait lengthened. Wannstedt's belly ached — and so did his jaw, having grown sore from nervous gum-chewing. Pitt said Wannstedt would have to leave

CAROLYN BAUMAN

Dallas in midstream and take the job by December 30. Johnson told Wannstedt the Cowboys could make adjustments, that he should take the job if he thought it was the best deal for his family.

On December 5, while the Cowboys were in Denver to play the Broncos, Wannstedt said to hell with five years, to hell with six or ten years. To hell with $1.5 million, and definitely to hell with leaving Johnson's Cowboys on a date they'd just be starting the NFL playoffs. What kind of friend would that be?

Wannstedt's allegiance paid off. Johnson again worked on his behalf a month later, when the Chicago Bears and New York Giants began a bidding war for Wannstedt's services. Like the dealers in one of his

★

"They were out to get me, but I still got a 'Shark' in at the end."

KENNY GANT
COWBOYS DEFENSIVE BACK
JANUARY 17, 1993

★

CAROLYN BAUMAN

Carolyn Bauman

Ron Jenkins

favorite card games, Johnson dealt a hand that gave Wannstedt and himself exactly what both wanted. Johnson got a trophy to mount on the wall, a protégé in bloom. (And one that would bloom outside of the NFC Eastern Division.) Wannstedt got a dream job, a five-year deal worth twice what Pitt had been offering a month earlier.

On Tuesday, January 19, 1993, the Wannstedts joined Bears president Mike McCaskey in the back of a limousine that would whiz them around town. During that ride, it struck Jan Wannstedt that her daughters would never again have the same relationship with Jimmy Johnson. And it struck Dave Wannstedt that it might be every seven months, instead of every seven days, when he could join Jimmy's gang filtering into On The Border.

Rodolfo Gonzalez

TEN

How Do You Top This?

The exclamation mark to two weeks of Super Bowl hype: Alvin Harper dunks the ball over the crossbar after scoring in the second half.

Days before the Dallas Cowboys are to play in Super Bowl XXVII, a rental car whizzes along the Pacific Coast Highway. Its driver spits tobacco juice into a cup. The disc jockey on the country-western radio station spits out bad Super Bowl jokes.

"What's the difference between a football and a gallstone?" the disc jockey asks. "Jim Kelly can pass a gallstone."

Aikman smiles slightly, curling his upper lip. "Don't laugh too hard," he says. "Come Sunday, they could be making that joke about me."

Bad prediction. Come Sunday, Aikman is the superstar on a Super team. He is going to Disney World (or Disneyland; he can't decide which). He is the nation's alarm clock on *Good Morning America* and its good-night kiss on *The Tonight Show*.

"He is going to be huge," says agent Leigh Steinberg, who, like some cartoon character, appears to have dollar signs in his eyes. Aikman hopes he can survive the

REX CURRY

Entrepreneurs find Cowboys fans hungry for all kinds of souvenirs in the days leading up to the game. For many, the Cowboys' trip to the Super Bowl is a first-time experience. Dallas last played in the game in 1979.

CAROLYN BAUMAN

Carolyn Bauman

Milton Adams

For one fan, emotion is written all over her face. For others, it is on their car windows.

PAUL MOSELEY

★

The Cowboys depart for Pasadena, California, under security worthy of a head of state. "We have to take this [game] as if we'll never be here again," Emmitt Smith says.

★

talk-show circuit without questions about his date with actress Janine Turner during Super Bowl Week or his polite turndown of an evening with singer Tanya Tucker, or any of the other glitzy slices of his life that conflict with the values he fights to hold onto. "Troy won't change," promises his mother, Charlyn. You look behind her back to see if her fingers are crossed.

As Aikman drives through the neighborhood of Westwood, he talks of visiting his old UCLA mentor, Bruins coach Terry Donahue. But there is a problem. The rental car lacks the proper permit, and Aikman is halted at the gate of a UCLA parking facility. The parking attendant asks for his name.

"Troy Aikman," he says.

Jerry Hoefer

The parking attendant does not blink. "Can't get in without a permit," she says.

Looking back, it seems preposterous to think someone wouldn't give Troy Aikman a key to the city, let alone a pass into a UCLA parking lot that might have been paid for with part of Aikman's $100,000 endowment. By the evening of Sunday, January 31, while Aikman and the Cowboys are kicking around the Buffalo Bills, the parking attendant is probably kicking herself in front of her television set.

Four days after the Super Bowl, the team that buried its egos and bonded from June to January has scattered. Jimmy Johnson has arranged to have the club announce his major coaching changes after his flight

★

Troy does L.A.: Despite the shades, the star quarterback cannot hide during media day at the Rose Bowl. But winning a date with actress Janine Turner of **Northern Exposure** *makes the week a little easier.*

★

for the Bahamas is off the ground. Dave Wannstedt is packing for Chicago. Six Cowboys, including Aikman, are in Hawaii for the Pro Bowl.

Downtown Julie Brown of MTV fame makes the most of Super Bowl Week, eliciting a kiss from Jimmy Johnson on media day, dancing with the Cowboys Cheerleaders the next.

Aikman spreads out a towel on Waikiki Beach on the island of Oahu. The discussion turns from what makes a good piña colada to his personal review of the 1992 Dallas Cowboys season. He talks about Dallas' surprisingly effective defense, about his warming relationship with Jimmy Johnson, about the dynamic presence of Jerry Jones, about Michael Irvin and Emmitt Smith and Jay Novacek and all the other weapons he has been surrounded with. And though he acknowledges how difficult it is to reach the pinnacle once, and

PAUL MOSELEY

Jerry Hoefer

how injuries and contract hassles and complacency and fate can conspire to kill defending champions, he talks about doing it all again in 1993.

"I've been thinking to myself, 'How do you top this?' " Aikman says. "But you know what? When a team has a year like this, you don't try to top it. You just try to match it."

★

Somewhere amidst the throng stands the head coach. Some 2,000-plus media representatives cover Super Bowl XXVII, which is broadcast to more than 100 countries.

★

Jerry Hoefer

Ron Jenkins

PAUL MOSELEY

Ready for the big date: A brilliant neon sign welcomes all to the Rose Bowl, built in 1922 and host to five Super Bowls; the gratis cushions for all ticket holders are neatly in place; and turf guru George Toma gives his fresh field a final trim.

Jerry Hoefer

COWBOYS
BILLS
DOWN
TO GO
BALL ON
Coca-Cola

Early in the week, a ticket on the 30-yard line, 50 rows up, sells for $1,500 in Los Angeles. By week's end, the price falls to $850.

JOYCE MARSHALL

Pages 156-157
A moment to himself: Jimmy Johnson watches pregame warm-ups at midfield.

BILLS
DOWN
TO GO
BALL ON

***

Early in the week, a ticket on the 30-yard line, 50 rows up, sells for $1,500 in Los Angeles. By week's end, the price falls to $850.

***

JOYCE MARSHALL

Pages 156-157
A moment to himself: Jimmy Johnson watches pregame warm-ups at midfield.

Paul Moseley

For autograph seekers, it's a target-rich environment: the best football players and a few good entertainers, too, such as Garth Brooks and Marlee Matlin.

Milton Adams

Ron Jenkins

Paul Moseley

JERRY HOEFER

Michael Irvin: "You dream about the moment. Then you win it and it becomes reality, and you can't put it into words."

James Washington: "As a kid you dream. And now I've got this. I've got a Super Bowl ring. And woooo-o-ooo, I feel good."

Emmitt Smith: "The greatest day of my life was being born. This is the second greatest day."

JERRY HOEFER

***

Is it the real Michael Jackson, or one of two impersonators who appear during the halftime extravaganza? During a 21-minute show, 3,500 children and teens join Jackson on the field as he entertains the Rose Bowl crowd with glitz and tricks, smoke and music.

***

Milton Adams

Paul Moseley

Jimmy Johnson receives the traditional victory dousing, but his hair doesn't move until Emmitt Smith comes around to muss it up.

Joyce Marshall

Ron Jenkins

JOYCE MARSHALL

The Cowboys take the second-half kickoff and drive for a field goal, putting to rest any hopes for a Buffalo revival. All that's left are the fireworks, inside and out.

Rex Curry

Ron Jenkins

FOR THE RECORD

Game-by-Game Summaries and 1992 Roster

EMMITT SMITH

ALL-PRO RUNNING BACK

SEASON RESULTS

Preseason

Date	Result	Rec.	Att.
Aug. 1	Oilers 34, Cowboys 23*	0-1	51,158
Aug. 7	Cowboys 27, Dolphins 24	1-1	50,803
Aug. 15	**Oilers 17, Cowboys 16**	**1-2**	**61,334**
Aug. 22	**Cowboys 17, Broncos 3**	**2-2**	**61,485**
Aug. 28	**Bears 20, Cowboys 13**	**2-3**	**60,218**

Regular season

Date	Result	Rec.	Att.
Sept. 7	**Cowboys 23, Redskins 10**	**1-0**	**63,538**
Sept. 13	Cowboys 34, Giants 28	2-0	76,430
Sept. 20	**Cowboys 31, Cardinals 20**	**3-0**	**62,575**
Sept. 27	open date		
Oct. 5	Eagles 31, Cowboys 7	3-1	66,572
Oct. 11	**Cowboys 27, Seahawks 0**	**4-1**	**62,311**
Oct. 18	**Cowboys 17, Chiefs 10**	**5-1**	**64,115**
Oct. 25	Cowboys 28, Raiders 13	6-1	91,505
Nov. 1	**Cowboys 20, Eagles 10**	**7-1**	**65,012**
Nov. 8	Cowboys 37, Lions 3	8-1	74,816
Nov. 15	**Rams 27, Cowboys 23**	**8-2**	**63,690**
Nov. 22	Cowboys 16, Cardinals 10	9-2	72,439
Nov. 26	**Cowboys 30, Giants 3**	**10-2**	**62,416**
Dec. 6	Cowboys 31, Broncos 27	11-2	74,946
Dec. 13	Redskins 20, Cowboys 17	11-3	56,437
Dec. 21	Cowboys 41, Falcons 17	12-3	67,036
Dec. 27	**Cowboys 27, Bears 14**	**13-3**	**63,101**

Postseason

Date	Result	Rec.	Att.
	NFC Divisional Playoff		
Jan. 10	**Cowboys 34, Eagles 10**	**14-3**	**63,721**
	NFC Championship		
Jan. 17	Cowboys 30, 49ers 20	15-3	64,920
	Super Bowl		
Jan. 31	Cowboys 52, Bills 17**	16-3	98,374

* — Played in Tokyo, Japan
** — Played in Pasadena, Calif.
Home games in bold

GAME 1: SEPT. 7

Cowboys 23, Redskins 10

Washington	**0**	**7**	**0**	**3—10**
Dallas	**9**	**7**	**7**	**0—23**

First quarter

Dal—Safety, Holt blocked punt out of end zone, 3:15

Dal—E. Smith 5 run (Elliott kick), 10:54

Second quarter

Was—Clark 30 pass from Rypien (Lohmiller kick), 10:12

Dal—Harper 26 pass from Aikman (Elliott kick), 13:58

Third quarter

Dal—Martin 79 punt return (Elliott kick), 9:18

Fourth quarter

Was—FG Lohmiller 51, 1:12

A—63,538.

Team statistics

	Was	Dal
First downs	17	23
Rushes-yards	22-75	35-174
Passing	189	216
Return Yards	59	87
Comp-Att-Int	20-38-0	18-31-2
Sacked-Yards Lost	2-19	0-0
Punts	7-43	4-49
Fumbles-Lost	2-1	0-0
Penalties-Yards	8-80	5-37
Time of Possession	26:47	33:13

Individual statistics

Rushing — Washington, Byner 13-58, Ervins 6-16, Monk 1-8, Rypien 1-0, Sanders 1-(-5). Dallas, E. Smith 26-139, Aikman 8-21, Johnston 1-14.

Passing — Washington, Rypien 20-38-0-208. Dallas, Aikman 18-31-2-216.

Receiving — Washington, Clark 8-97, Byner 4-31, Sanders 3-20, Monk 2-43, Ervins 2-12, Warren 1-5. Dallas, Irvin 5-89, Johnston 4-39, Harper 3-59, E. Smith 3-13, Martin 2-12, Novacek 1-4.

GAME 2: SEPT. 13

Cowboys 34, Giants 28

Dallas	**17**	**10**	**7**	**0—34**
New York	**0**	**0**	**14**	**14—28**

First quarter

Dal—E. Smith 5 run (Elliott kick), 4:11

Dal—Williams 3 blocked punt return (Elliott kick), 6:41

Dal—FG Elliott 39, 13:37

Second quarter

Dal—FG Elliott 35, :57

Dal—Novacek 2 pass from Aikman (Elliott kick), 14:28

Third quarter

Dal—Irvin 27 pass from Aikman (Elliott kick), 1:30

NY—Hampton 5 run (Bahr kick), 5:53

NY—Bunch 1 pass from Simms (Bahr kick), 14:25

Fourth quarter

NY—Baker 6 pass from Simms (Bahr kick), 4:35

NY—Cross 2 pass from Simms (Bahr kick), 8:08

A—76,430.

Team statistics

	Dal	NY
First downs	20	22
Rushes-yards	26-98	18-67
Passing	229	264
Return Yards	122	102
Comp-Att-Int	22-35-0	25-42-1
Sacked-Yards Lost	2-9	2-9
Punts	6-42	6-35
Fumbles-Lost	0-0	0-0
Penalties-Yards	7-45	5-43
Time of Possession	31:21	28:39

Individual statistics

Rushing — Dallas, E. Smith 23-89, Aikman 2-8, Johnston 1-1. New York, Hampton 17-64, Simms 1-3.

Passing — Dallas, Aikman 22-35-0-238. New York, Simms 25-42-1-273.

Receiving — Dallas, E. Smith 8-55, Novacek 5-33, Irvin 4-73, Martin 2-41, Roberts 1-18, Harper 1-11, Johnson 1-7. New York, Cross 6-77, McCaffrey 5-82, Hampton 5-36, Calloway 2-23, Bunch 2-7, Meggett 2-(-1), Smith 1-22, Ingram 1-21, Baker 1-6.

GAME 3: SEPT. 20

Cowboys 31, Cardinals 20

Phoenix	**7**	**3**	**3**	**7—20**
Dallas	**14**	**7**	**7**	**3—31**

First quarter

Dal—Irvin 87 pass from Aikman (Elliott kick), 1:01

Pho—Hill 34 pass from Chandler (Davis kick), 10:13

Dal—Irvin 41 pass from Aikman (Elliott kick), 14:40

Second quarter

Dal—E. Smith 1 run (Elliott kick), 11:30

Pho—FG Davis 22, 13:37

Third quarter

Dal—Irvin 4 pass from Aikman (Elliott kick), 7:32

Pho—FG Davis 42, 10:51

Fourth quarter

Dal—FG Elliott 29, 7:02

Pho—Brown 1 run (Davis kick), 10:13

A—62,575.

Team statistics

	Pho	Dal
First downs	24	21
Rushes-yards	17-67	38-150
Passing	371	263
Return Yards	130	9
Comp-Att-Int	28-43-0	14-21-0
Sacked-Yards Lost	2-12	0-0
Punts	2-52	3-51
Fumbles-Lost	2-2	0-0
Penalties-Yards	6-37	3-14
Time of Possession	25:59	34:01

Individual statistics

Rushing — Phoenix, Brown 12-31, Bailey 2-22, Chandler 2-12, Centers 1-2. Dallas, E. Smith 26-112, Richards 7-32, Johnston 3-7, Aikman 1-8, Irvin 1-(-9).

Passing — Phoenix, Chandler 28-43-0-383. Dallas, Aikman 14-21-0-263.

Receiving — Phoenix, Centers 7-64, Jones 5-78, Proehl 4-51, Rolle 4-19, Bailey 3-53, Hill 2-74, Brown 2-31, Johnson 1-13. Dallas, Irvin 8-210, Novacek 3-28, Harper 1-14, Martin 1-7, Richards 1-4.

GAME 4: OCT. 5

Eagles 31, Cowboys 7

Dallas	**7**	**0**	**0**	**0—7**
Philadelphia	**10**	**0**	**7**	**14—31**

First quarter

Phi—Cunningham 2 run (Ruzek kick), 3:15

Dal—Martin 7 pass from Aikman (Elliott kick), 7:05

Phi—FG Ruzek 40, 13:26

Third quarter

Phi—Walker 9 run (Ruzek kick), 14:59

Fourth quarter

Phi—Walker 16 run (Ruzek kick), 3:20

Phi—Byars 12 run (Ruzek kick), 11:56

A—66,572.

Team statistics

	Dal	Phi
First downs	17	21
Rushes-yards	22-80	32-160
Passing	231	106
Return Yards	118	73
Comp-Att-Int	19-38-3	11-19-1
Sacked-Yards Lost	4-25	2-18
Punts	4-41	4-53
Fumbles-Lost	1-1	1-0
Penalties-Yards	9-58	4-30
Time of Possession	29:15	30:45

Individual statistics

Rushing — Dallas, E. Smith 19-67, Agee 2-11, Johnston 1-2. Philadelphia, Walker 19-86, Byars 8-25, Cunningham 7-43, Sherman 2-6.

Passing — Dallas, Aikman 19-38-3-256. Philadelphia, Cunningham 11-19-1-124.

Receiving — Dallas, Novacek 6-61, Irvin 4-105, Martin 3-31, E. Smith 2-5, Harper 1-42, Gesek 1-4, Roberts 1-4, Agee 1-4. Philadelphia, Barnett 5-76, Walker 3-14, Byars 1-14, Williams 1-13, Beach 1-7.

GAME 5: OCT. 11

Cowboys 27, Seahawks 0

Seattle	**0**	**0**	**0**	**0— 0**
Dallas	**7**	**13**	**7**	**0—27**

First quarter

Dal—E. Smith 2 run (Elliott kick), 3:43

Second quarter

Dal—E. Smith 1 run (Elliott kick), 5:36

Dal—FG Elliott 31, 8:12

Dal—FG Elliott 51, 13:09

Third quarter

Dal—Horton 15 interception return (Elliott kick), 10:16

A—62,311.

Team statistics

	Sea	**Dal**
First downs	6	16
Rushes-yards	22-38	30-116
Passing	24	197
Return Yards	135	26
Comp-Att-Int	8-19-1	17-28-2
Sacked-Yards Lost	7-54	1-3
Punts	8-49	5-46
Fumbles-Lost	3-2	0-0
Penalties-Yards	7-40	3-15
Time of Possession	26:44	33:16

Individual statistics

Rushing — Seattle, Warren 7-14, Williams 8-10, Mayes 4-12, McGwire 2-2, Gelbaugh 1-0. Dallas, E. Smith 22-78, Johnston 4-9, Agee 3-10, Aikman 1-19.

Passing — Seattle, McGwire 5-9-0-46, Gelbaugh 3-10-1-33. Dallas, Aikman 15-23-2-173, Beuerlein 2-5-0-27.

Receiving — Seattle, Thomas 3-28, Williams 3-24, Daniels 1-15, Thomas 1-12. Dallas, Irvin 6-113, Novacek 5-22, Harper 5-20, Martin 4-45.

MARK STEPNOSKI

ALL-PRO CENTER

GAME 8: NOV. 1

Cowboys 20, Eagles 10

Philadelphia	**0**	**0**	**10**	**0—10**
Dallas	**0**	**3**	**7**	**10—20**

Second quarter

Dal—FG Elliott 35, 14:39

Third quarter

Phi—Walker 2 run (Ruzek kick), 4:36

Dal—Martin 22 pass from Aikman (Elliott kick), 7:27

Phi—FG Ruzek 18, 13:05

Fourth quarter

Dal—FG Elliott 48, :05

Dal—Johnston 14 pass from Aikman (Elliott kick), 7:21

A—65,012.

Team statistics

	Phi	**Dal**
First downs	9	22
Rushes-yards	21-73	35-175
Passing	117	214
Return Yards	52	76
Comp-Att-Int	13-27-2	19-33-1
Sacked-Yards Lost	2-18	1-0
Punts	8-46	5-34
Fumbles-Lost	0-0	1-1
Penalties-Yards	5-31	5-28
Time of Possession	24:40	35:20

Individual statistics

Rushing — Philadelphia, Walker 16-44, McMahon 2-21, Byars 2-5, Cunningham 1-3. Dallas, E. Smith 30-163, Aikman 4-11, Johnston 1-1.

Passing — Philadelphia, Cunningham 3-8-1-13, McMahon 10-19-1-122. Dallas, Aikman 19-33-1-214.

Receiving — Philadelphia, Byars 6-37, Williams 2-54, Walker 2-5, Barnett 1-15, Green 1-13, Sikahema 1-11. Dallas, Martin 7-83, Johnston 4-46, Novacek 4-38, Irvin 2-29, E. Smith 1-9, Harper 1-9.

GAME 6: OCT. 18

Cowboys 17, Chiefs 10

Kansas City	**3**	**7**	**0**	**0—10**
Dallas	**7**	**7**	**3**	**0—17**

First quarter

KC—FG Lowery 32, 8:30

Dal—Johnston 2 pass from Aikman (Elliott kick), 13:57

Second quarter

Dal—E. Smith 2 run (Elliott kick), 3:55

KC—Word 2 run (Lowery kick), 13:03

Third quarter

Dal—FG Elliott 39, 7:36

A—64,115.

Team statistics

	KC	**Dal**
First downs	18	17
Rushes-yards	25-91	24-95
Passing	139	183
Return Yards	115	84
Comp-Att-Int	16-31-1	21-29-2
Sacked-Yards Lost	3-31	1-9
Punts	6-39	4-46
Fumbles-Lost	1-0	0-0
Penalties-Yards	5-54	11-74
Time of Possession	30:47	29:13

Individual statistics

Rushing — Kansas City, Word 13-46, Williams 6-28, Okoye 5-17, Krieg 1-0. Dallas, E. Smith 24-95.

Passing — Kansas City, Krieg 16-31-1-170. Dallas, Aikman 21-29-2-192.

Receiving — Kansas City, Davis 6-100, McNair 3-16, Jones 2-24, Birden 1-10, Harry 1-7, Hayes 1-6, Word 1-5, Anders 1-2. Dallas, Irvin 6-84, Novacek 5-36, Johnston 5-29, E. Smith 4-35, Agee 1-8.

GAME 7: OCT. 25

Cowboys 28, Raiders 13

Dallas	**7**	**0**	**7**	**14—28**
Los Angeles	**6**	**0**	**7**	**0—13**

First quarter

LA—Allen 1 run (pass failed), 4:40

Dal—E. Smith 6 run (Elliott kick), 13:28

Third quarter

LA—Gault 31 pass from Marinovich (Jaeger kick), 4:18

Dal—E. Smith 4 run (Elliott kick), 7:23

Fourth quarter

Dal—Aikman 3 run (Elliott kick), 4:54

Dal—E. Smith 26 run (Elliott kick), 11:34

A—91,505.

Team statistics

	Dal	**LA**
First downs	23	12
Rushes-yards	39-162	20-71
Passing	207	94
Return Yards	87	120
Comp-Att-Int	16-25-0	8-26-0
Sacked-Yards Lost	5-27	3-23
Punts	5-37	6-45
Fumbles-Lost	2-0	2-1
Penalties-Yards	7-56	5-28
Time of Possession	37:17	22:43

Individual statistics

Rushing — Dallas, Smith 29-152, Aikman 8-4, Johnston 1-4, Richards 1-2. Los Angeles, Dickerson 8-42, Smith 4-7, Allen 3-9, Schroeder 2-5, Bell 2-4, Marinovich 1-4.

Passing — Dallas, Aikman 16-25-0-234. Los Angeles, Marinovich 8-23-0-117, Schroeder 0-3-0-0.

Receiving — Dallas, Harper 4-79, Novacek 3-60, Irvin 3-54, E. Smith 3-15, Johnston 2-11, Martin 1-15. Los Angeles, Brown 2-28, Smith 2-13, Gault 1-31, Horton 1-26, Glover 1-10, Fernandez 1-9.

GAME 9: NOV. 8

Cowboys 37, Lions 3

Dallas	**14**	**6**	**14**	**3—37**
Detroit	**0**	**3**	**0**	**0— 3**

First quarter

Dal—E. Smith 7 run (Elliott kick), 12:22

Dal—E. Smith 1 run (Elliott kick), 14:51

Second quarter

Det—FG Hanson 36, 5:48

Dal—FG Elliott 25, 13:34

Dal—FG Elliott 42, 14:57

Third quarter

Dal—E. Smith 1 run (Elliott kick), 2:33

Dal—Irvin 14 pass from Aikman (Elliott kick), 14:47

Fourth quarter

Dal—FG Elliott 30, 14:40

A—74,816.

Team statistics

	Dal	**Det**
First downs	26	10
Rushes-yards	37-158	22-124
Passing	240	77
Return Yards	105	199
Comp-Att-Int	18-27-1	9-17-3
Sacked-Yards Lost	0-0	2-13
Punts	2-46	5-37
Fumbles-Lost	1-1	2-1
Penalties-Yards	3-15	10-69
Time of Possession	37:57	22:03

Individual statistics

Rushing — Dallas, E. Smith 19-67, Richards 16-82, Martin 1-8, Agee 1-1. Detroit, Sanders 18-108, Peete 2-9, Kramer 1-6, Stradford 1-1.

Passing — Dallas, Aikman 16-25-1-214, Beuerlein 2-2-0-26. Detroit, Peete 6-10-2-69, Kramer 3-7-1-21.

Receiving — Dallas, Irvin 5-114, Harper 3-61, Novacek 3-29, E. Smith 3-13, Johnston 3-9, Roberts 1-14. Detroit, Moore 4-57, Farr 2-14, Campbell 1-10, Perriman 1-6, Sanders 1-3.

GAME 10: NOV. 15

Rams 27, Cowboys 23

Los Angeles	**7**	**14**	**0**	**6—27**
Dallas	**3**	**10**	**10**	**0—23**

First quarter

LA—Gary 1 run (Zendejas kick), 7:10

Dal—FG Elliott 37, 10:44

Second quarter

Dal—E. Smith 3 run (Elliott kick), :34

Dal—FG Elliott 42, 6:59

LA—Chadwick 8 pass from Everett (Zendejas kick), 12:45

LA—Gary 3 pass from Everett (Zendejas kick), 14:42

Third quarter

Dal—FG Elliott 36, 5:02

Dal—Martin 74 punt return (Elliott kick), 13:49

Fourth quarter

LA—FG Zendejas 33, 4:31

LA—FG Zendejas 44, 13:06

A—63,690.

Team statistics

	LA	Dal
First downs	24	19
Rushes-yards	32-123	19-80
Passing	244	269
Return Yards	56	177
Comp-Att-Int	22-37-0	22-37-0
Sacked-Yards Lost	1-7	1-3
Punts	4-37	3-43
Fumbles-Lost	0-0	1-0
Penalties-Yards	2-10	7-60
Time of Possession	33:28	26:32

Individual statistics

Rushing — Los Angeles, Gary 29-110, Everett 1-6, Turner 1-5, Thompson 1-2. Dallas, E. Smith 19-80.

Passing — Los Angeles, Everett 22-37-0-251. Dallas, Aikman 22-37-0-272.

Receiving — Los Angeles, Gary 7-44, Chadwick 4-38, Anderson 3-77, Cox 2-26, Carter 2-26, Ellard 2-23, Price 1-10, Lang 1-7. Dallas, Irvin 8-168, Novacek 5-27, Martin 4-51, Johnston 2-13, E. Smith 2-8, Harper 1-5.

NATE NEWTON

ALL-PRO GUARD

GAME 13: DEC. 6

Cowboys 31, Broncos 27

Dallas	**14**	**3**	**7**	**7—31**
Denver	**7**	**6**	**7**	**7—27**

First quarter

Dal—Irvin 6 pass from Aikman (Elliott kick), 3:45

Dal—Irvin 4 pass from Aikman (Elliott kick), 6:58

Den—Johnson 18 pass from Maddox (Treadwell kick), 12:29

Second quarter

Den—Jackson 12 pass from Maddox (run failed), :47

Dal—FG Elliott 53, 11:35

Third quarter

Dal—Novacek 1 pass from Aikman (Elliott kick), 6:38

Den—Rivers 23 pass from Maddox (Treadwell kick), 12:55

Fourth quarter

Den—Tillman 81 pass from Marshall (Treadwell kick), 5:55

Dal—E. Smith 3 run (Elliott kick), 12:13

A—79,946.

Team statistics

	Dal	Den
First downs	22	15
Rushes-yards	32-82	19-93
Passing	222	261
Return Yards	61	104
Comp-Att-Int	25-35-0	18-31-4
Sacked-Yards Lost	2-9	4-28
Punts	4-46	2-49
Fumbles-Lost	2-0	2-1
Penalties-Yards	7-35	7-67
Time of Possession	37:47	22:13

Individual statistics

Rushing — Dallas, E. Smith 26-62, Aikman 6-20. Denver, Lewis 10-59, Moore 4-24, Rivers 3-8, Maddox 2-2.

Passing — Dallas, Aikman 25-35-0-231. Denver, Maddox 10-17-4-104, Moore 7-13-0-104, Marshall 1-1-0-81.

Receiving — Dallas, Novacek 7-87, Irvin 6-62, E. Smith 6-45, Johnston 3-18, Harper 2-17, Martin 1-2. Denver, Johnson 4-71, Rivers 4-38, Jackson 3-39, Sharpe 3-16, Lewis 2-25, Tillman 1-81, Marshall 1-19.

GAME 11: NOV. 22

Cowboys 16, Cardinals 10

Dallas	**0**	**10**	**6**	**0—16**
Phoenix	**7**	**0**	**0**	**3—10**

First quarter

Pho—Centers 2 pass from Chandler (Davis kick), 8:29

Second quarter

Dal—FG Elliott 28, 7:09

Dal—Novacek 7 pass from Aikman (Elliott kick), 14:46

Third quarter

Dal—Harper 37 pass from Aikman (kick failed), 12:32

Fourth quarter

Pho—FG Davis 20, 11:12

A—72,439.

Team statistics

	Dal	Pho
First downs	18	9
Rushes-yards	30-97	18-46
Passing	237	103
Return Yards	81	165
Comp-Att-Int	25-36-1	15-24-0
Sacked-Yards Lost	0-0	2-15
Punts	5-39	6-44
Fumbles-Lost	0-0	2-1
Penalties-Yards	5-40	5-34
Time of Possession	36:09	23:51

Individual statistics

Rushing — Dallas, E. Smith 23-84, Aikman 4-6, Johnston 2-6, Richards 1-1. Phoenix, Johnson 12-45, Rosenbach 4-0, Bailey 2-1.

Passing — Dallas, Aikman 25-36-1-237. Phoenix, Chandler 5-7-0-38, Rosenbach 10-17-0-80.

Receiving — Dallas, E. Smith 12-67, Harper 5-88, Novacek 5-50, Irvin 1-18, Johnston 1-8, Martin 1-6. Phoenix, Centers 5-28, Edwards 3-24, Johnson 2-12, Bailey 1-34, Hill 1-18, Rolle 1-2.

GAME 12: NOV. 26

Cowboys 30, Giants 3

New York	**0**	**3**	**0**	**0— 3**
Dallas	**3**	**6**	**14**	**7—30**

First quarter

Dal—FG Elliott 45, 11:38

Second quarter

Dal—FG Elliott 33, 2:21

Dal—FG Elliott 53, 12:38

NY—FG Bahr 42, 14:57

Third quarter

Dal—E. Smith 26 pass from Aikman (Elliott kick), 8:57

Dal—E. Smith 68 run (Elliott kick), 11:07

Fourth quarter

Dal—Harper 4 pass from Aikman (Elliott kick), 8:56

A—62,416.

Team statistics

	NY	Dal
First downs	12	7
Rushes-yards	22-80	30-157
Passing	127	142
Return Yards	123	85
Comp-Att-Int	14-31-0	19-29-1
Sacked-Yards Lost	4-30	1-1
Punts	8-37	3-45
Fumbles-Lost	2-1	0-0
Penalties-Yards	11-80	7-68
Time of Possession	25:24	34:36

Individual statistics

Rushing — New York, Hampton 10-33, Bunch 6-20, Meggett 3-22, Graham 2-4, Brown 1-1. Dallas, E. Smith 17-120, Richards 8-32, Aikman 2-7, Beuerlein 2-(-3), Johnston 1-1.

Passing — New York, Graham 12-28-0-151, Brown 2-3-0-6. Dallas, Aikman 19-29-1-143.

Receiving — New York, McCaffrey 6-105, Calloway 2-15, Hampton 2-13, Meggett 2-13, Cross 2-11. Dallas, E. Smith 6-41, Irvin 4-37, Johnston 3-30, Novacek 3-22, Harper 2-15, Richards 1-(-2)

GAME 14: DEC. 13

Redskins 20, Cowboys 17

Dallas	**3**	**14**	**0**	**0—17**
Washington	**0**	**7**	**3**	**10—20**

First quarter

Dal—FG Elliott 23, 9:57

Second quarter

Dal—Novacek 5 pass from Aikman (Elliott kick), 4:51

Was—Orr 41 pass from Byner (Lohmiller kick), 6:47

Dal—Novacek 5 pass from Aikman (Elliott kick), 14:51

Third quarter

Was—FG Lohmiller 32, 10:01

Fourth quarter

Was—FG Lohmiller 22, 7:58

Was—Copeland recovered fumble in end zone (Lohmiller kick), 11:46

A—56,437.

Team statistics

	Dal	Was
First downs	22	14
Rushes-yards	29-121	25-68
Passing	221	178
Return Yards	109	130
Comp-Att-Int	23-35-1	13-30-1
Sacked-Yards Lost	4-24	2-7
Punts	4-40	5-37
Fumbles-Lost	4-3	0-0
Penalties-Yards	5-37	6-56
Time of Possession	32:14	27:46

Individual statistics

Rushing — Dallas, E. Smith 25-99, Johnston 2-16, Martin 1-5, Aikman 1-1. Washington, Byner 19-69, Rypien 3-(-4), Ervins 2-0, Sanders 1-3.

Passing — Dallas, Aikman 23-35-1-245. Washington, Rypien 12-29-1-144, Byner 1-1-0-41.

Receiving — Dallas, Irvin 5-105, Novacek 5-25, E. Smith 5-16, Harper 4-51, Martin 3-33, Johnston 1-15. Washington, Clark 4-50, Sanders 3-53, Orr 2-46, Byner 2-19, Monk 1-9, Ervins 1-8.

GAME 15: DEC. 21

Cowboys 41, Falcons 17

Dallas	**3**	**17**	**14**	**7—41**
Atlanta	**7**	**3**	**0**	**7—17**

First quarter

Dal—FG Elliott 47, 5:29.

Atl—Hill 6 pass from Wilson (Johnson kick), 9:39.

Second quarter

Dal—Martin 11 pass from Aikman (Elliott kick), :53.

Dal—FG Elliott 22, 8:46.

Dal—Novacek 18 pass from Aikman (Elliott kick), 13:46.

Atl—FG Johnson 27, 15:00.

Third quarter

Dal—Harper 23 pass from Aikman (Elliott kick), 3:10.

Dal—E.Smith 29 run (Elliott kick), 3:35.

Fourth quarter

Dal—E.Smith 29 run (Elliott kick), 2:45.

Atl—Rison 10 pass from Wilson (Johnson kick), 6:45.

A—67,036.

Team statistics

	Dal	Atl
First downs	19	18
Rushes-yards	29-196	11-40
Passing	239	335
Return Yards	11	13
Comp-Att-Int	18-21-0	34-46-0
Sacked-Yards Lost	0-0	4-37
Punts	2-53	2-50
Fumbles-Lost	0-0	4-3
Penalties-Yards	7-50	3-24
Time of Possession	33:05	26:55

Individual statistics

Rushing — Dallas, E. Smith 24-174, Harper 1-15, Richards 3-5, Agee 1-2. Atlanta, Broussard 4-17, Wilson 2-15, T. Smith 2-9, K.Jones 2-3, Sanders 1-(-4).

Passing — Dallas, Aikman 18-21-0-239. Atlanta, Wilson 30-41-0-342, Tolliver 4-5-0-30.

Receiving — Dallas, Irvin 6-89, Novacek 5-69, Harper 3-53, Martin 2-23, E. Smith 2-5. Atlanta, Pritchard 9-105, Hill 9-84, Rison 6-45, Haynes 5-100, K. Jones 2-21, Broussard 2-12, Milling 1-5.

GAME 16: DEC. 27

Cowboys 27, Bears 14

Chicago	**0**	**0**	**0**	**14—14**
Dallas	**0**	**3**	**24**	**0—27**

Second Quarter

Dal—FG Elliott 21, 13:56.

Third Quarter

Dal—E.Smith 31 run (Elliott kick), 3:55.

Dal—Maryland 26 fumble return (Elliott kick), 4:26.

Dal—Richards 3 run (Elliott kick), 8:49.

Dal—FG Elliott 34, 13:48.

Fourth Quarter

Chi—Green 6 run (Butler kick), 2:30.

Chi—Zorich 42 fumble return (Butler kick), 5:41.

A—63,101.

	Chi	Dal
First downs	9	22
Rushes-yards	15-28	44-179
Passing	64	175
Return Yards	32	80
Comp-Att-Int	9-23-3	18-31-1
Sacked-Yards Lost	2-25	1-2
Punts	7-44	2-44
Fumbles-Lost	2-1	4-3
Penalties-Yards	6-50	1-15
Time of Possession	18:01	41:59

Individual statistics

Rushing — Chicago, Anderson 3-17, Green 3-11, Muster 2-5, Lewis 7-(minus 5). Dallas, E.Smith 20-131, Agee 9-30, Richards 13-22, Beuerlein 2-(minus 4).

Passing — Chicago, Furrer 9-23-3-89. Dallas, Aikman 10-20-0-78, Beuerlein 8-11-1-99.

Receiving — Chicago, Morgan 5-53, Jennings 2-17, Davis 1-13, Lewis 1-6. Dallas, Irvin 5-46, Novacek 3-39, Johnston 3-24, Harper 2-38, E.Smith 2-8, Martin 1-10, Agee 1-6, Richards 1-6.

DIVISIONAL PLAYOFF: JAN. 10

Cowboys 34, Eagles 10

Philadelphia	**3**	**0**	**0**	**7—10**
Dallas	**7**	**10**	**10**	**7—34**

First Quarter

Phi—FG Ruzek 32, 7:15.

Dal—Tennell 1 pass from Aikman (Elliott kick), 13:02.

Second Quarter

Dal—Novacek 6 pass from Aikman (Elliott kick), 14:13.

Dal—FG Elliott 20, 15:00.

Third Quarter

Dal—E.Smith 23 run (Elliott kick), 3:44.

Dal—FG Elliott 43, 11:43.

Fourth Quarter

Dal—Gainer 1 run (Elliott kick), 11:41.

Phi—C.Williams 18 pass from Cunningham (Ruzek kick), 14:10.

A—63,721.

	Phi	Dal
First downs	12	22
Rushes-yards	17-63	38-160
Passing	115	186
Return Yards	24	5
Comp-Att-Int	17-30-0	15-25-0
Sacked-Yards Lost	5-45	2-14
Punts	7-41	4-43
Fumbles-Lost	4-2	2-1
Penalties-Yards	6-76	5-30
Time of Possession	24:43	35:17

Individual statistics

Rushing — Philadelphia, Walker 6-29, Cunningham 5-22, Sherman 6-12. Dallas, E.Smith 25-114, Gainer 9-29, Aikman 3-13, Johnston 1-4.

Passing — Philadelphia, Cunningham 17-30-0-160. Dallas, Aikman 15-25-0-200.

Receiving — Philadelphia, Walker 6-37, C.Williams 4-48, Barnett 4-44, Byars 3-31. Dallas, Irvin 6-88, Novacek 3-36, Martin 3-27, Harper 1-41, Johnston 1-7, Tennell 1-1.

Missed field goals—None.

CONFERENCE CHAMPIONSHIP: JAN. 17

Cowboys 30, 49ers 20

Dallas	**3**	**7**	**7**	**13—30**
San Francisco	**7**	**3**	**3**	**7—20**

First Quarter

Dal—FG Elliott 20, 8:20.

SF—Young 1 run (Cofer kick), 11:11.

Second Quarter

Dal—E.Smith 5 run (Elliott kick), 9:55.

SF—FG Cofer 28, 13:41.

Third Quarter

Dal—Johnston 4 run (Elliott kick), 4:15.

SF—FG Cofer 42, 8:35.

Fourth Quarter

Dal—E.Smith 16 pass from Aikman (Elliott kick), 2:35.

SF—Rice 5 pass from Young (Cofer kick), 10:38.

Dal—K.Martin 6 pass from Aikman (kick failed), 11:17.

A—64,920.

	Dal	SF
First downs	24	24
Rushes-yards	30-121	21-114
Passing	295	301
Return Yards	43	30
Comp-Att-Int	24-34-0	25-35-2
Sacked-Yards Lost	4-27	3-12
Punts	4-36	1-57
Fumbles-Lost	1-0	2-2
Penalties-Yards	4-25	4-38
Time of Possession	35:20	24:40

Individual statistics

Rushing — Dallas, E.Smith 24-114, Johnston 2-7, Harper 1-3, Aikman 3-(minus 3). San Francisco, Watters 11-69, Young 8-33, Rathman 1-6, Lee 1-6.

Passing — Dallas, Aikman 24-34-0-322. San Francisco, Young 25-35-2-313.

Receiving — Dallas, E.Smith 7-59, Irvin 6-86, Johnston 4-26, Harper 3-117, Novacek 3-28, K.Martin 1-6. San Francisco, Rice 8-123, Watters 6-69, Rathman 4-33, Jones 3-40, Taylor 3-33, Sherrard 1-15.

Missed field goals — Dallas, Elliott 43. San Francisco, Cofer 47.

TROY AIKMAN

ALL-PRO QUARTERBACK • SUPER BOWL XXVII MVP

SUPER BOWL: JAN. 31

Cowboys 52, Bills 17

Buffalo	**7**	**3**	**7**	**0—17**
Dallas	**14**	**14**	**3**	**21—52**

First quarter

Buf—Thomas 2 run (Christie kick), 5:00.

Dal—Novacek 23 pass from Aikman (Elliott kick), 13:24.

Dal—J.Jones 2 fumble return (Elliott kick), 13:39.

Second quarter

Buf—FG Christie 21, 11:36.

Dal—Irvin 19 pass from Aikman (Elliott kick), 13:06.

Dal—Irvin 18 pass from Aikman (Elliott kick), 13:24.

Third quarter

Dal—FG Elliott 20, 6:39.

Buf—Beebe 40 pass from Reich (Christie kick), 15:00.

Fourth quarter

Dal—Harper 45 pass from Aikman (Elliott kick), 4:56.

Dal—E.Smith 10 run (Elliott kick), 6:48.

Dal—Norton 9 fumble return (Elliott kick), 7:29.

A—98,374. No-shows—0.

	Buf	**Dal**
First downs	22	20
Rushing	7	9
Passing	11	11
Penalty	4	0
Third down eff.	5-11	5-11
Fourth down eff.	0-2	0-1
Total net yards	362	408
Total Plays	71	60
Avg Gain	5.1	6.8
Net yards rushing	108	137
Rushes	29	29
Avg per rush	3.7	4.7
Net yards passing	254	271
Completed-Att.	22-38	22-30
Yards-Pass Play	6.0	8.7
Sacked-Yds lost	4-22	1-2
Had Intercepted	4	0
Punts-Avg.	3-45	4-33
Total return yardage	90	149
Punts Returns	1-0	3-35
Kickoffs Returns	4-90	4-79
Interceptions	0-0	4-35
Penalties-Yds	4-30	8-53
Fumbles-Lost	8-5	4-2
Time of possession	28:48	31:12

Individual statistics

Rushing: Buffalo—K.Davis 15-86, Thomas 11-19, Gardner 1-3, Reich 2-0. **Dallas**—E.Smith 22-108, Aikman 3-28, Gainer 2-1, Johnston 1-0, Beuerlein 1-0.

Passing: Buffalo—Kelly 4-7-2-82, Reich 18-31-2-194. **Dallas**—Aikman 22-30-0-273.

Receiving: Buffalo—Reed 8-152, Thomas 4-10, K.Davis 3-16, Beebe 2-50, Tasker 2-30, Metzelaars 2-12, McKeller 1-6. **Dallas**—Novacek 7-72, Irvin 6-114, E.Smith 6-27, Johnston 2-15, Harper 1-45.

Tackles-assists-sacks: Buffalo—Bennett 8-1-0, Talley 6-0-0, Patton 6-0-0, B.Smith 4-1-1, Odomes 4-0-0, Conlan 3-5-0, Jones 3-2-0, Williams 3-2-0, Darby 3-0-0, Wright 3-0-0, Pike 3-0-0, Kelso 2-2-0, Hanson 2-1-0, Hale 2-0-0, Maddox 1-0-0, K.Davis 1-0-0, Beebe 1-0-0, Metzelaars 1-0-0, Tasker 0-1-0, Goganious 0-1-0. **Dallas** — Norton 8-1-0, Haley 5-0-1, Washington 4-2-0, Edwards 4-2-0, Maryland 4-2-0, Woodson 4-0-0, Lett 3-0-1, Everett 3-0-1, Holmes 3-0-0, Casillas 2-3-0, Jeffcoat 2-0-1, Brown 2-0-0, V.Smith 2-0-0, R.Jones 2-0-0, Gant 2-1-0, Horton 1-0-0, K.Smith 1-0-0, Holt 1-0-0, Tolbert 1-0-0, Gainer 1-0-0, Pruitt 1-0-0.

Interceptions: Buffalo—None. **Dallas**—Everett 2, Brown, Washington.

Missed field goals: Buffalo — None. **Dallas** — None.

Officials: Referee Dick Hantak, Ump Ron Botchan, HL Ron Phares, LJ Dick McKenzie, BJ Jim Poole, SJ Dean Look, FJ Donnie Hampton.

Time: 3:23.

COWBOYS ROSTER

No.	Player	Pos.	Ht.	Wt.	Age	Exp.	College
2	Lin Elliott	K	6-0	182	24	R	Texas Tech
4	Mike Saxon	P	6-3	200	30	8	San Diego State
7	Steve Beuerlein	QB	6-2	213	27	5	Notre Dame
8	Troy Aikman	QB	6-4	222	26	4	UCLA
20	Ray Horton	S	5-11	188	32	10	Washington
22	Emmitt Smith	RB	5-9	209	23	3	Florida
23	Robert Williams	S	5-10	186	30	6	Baylor
24	Larry Brown	CB	5-11	185	23	2	TCU
26	Kevin Smith	CB	5-11	177	22	R	Texas A&M
27	Thomas Everett	S	5-9	183	28	6	Baylor
28	Darren Woodson	S	6-1	215	23	R	Arizona State
29	Kenneth Gant	S	5-11	191	25	3	Albany State
30	Issiac Holt	CB	6-2	198	30	8	Alcorn State
34	Tommie Agee	FB	6-0	227	28	5	Auburn
37	James Washington	S	6-1	203	28	5	UCLA
39	Derrick Gainer	RB	5-11	240	26	2	Florida A&M
47	Clayton Holmes	CB	5-10	181	23	R	Carson-Newman
48	Daryl Johnston	FB	6-2	238	26	4	Syracuse
51	Ken Norton Jr.	LB	6-2	241	26	5	UCLA
52	Mickey Pruitt	LB	6-1	218	28	5	Colorado
53	Mark Stepnoski	C	6-2	269	25	4	Pittsburgh
55	Robert Jones	LB	6-2	238	23	R	East Carolina
57	Vinson Smith	LB	6-2	237	27	4	East Carolina
58	Dixon Edwards	LB	6-1	224	24	2	Michigan State
61	Nate Newton	G	6-3	303	31	7	Florida A&M
63	John Gesek	G	6-5	282	29	6	Cal.-Sacramento
66	Kevin Gogan	G/T	6-7	319	28	6	Washington
67	Russell Maryland	DT	6-1	275	23	2	Miami, Fla.
68	Frank Cornish	C/G	6-4	285	25	3	UCLA
70	Dale Hellestrae	G/C	6-5	283	30	6	SMU
71	Mark Tuinei	T	6-5	298	32	10	Hawaii
75	Tony Casillas	DT	6-3	273	29	7	Oklahoma
76	Alan Veingrad	G/T	6-5	280	29	6	East Texas State
77	Jim Jeffcoat	DE	6-5	276	31	10	Arizona State
78	Leon Lett	DL	6-6	292	24	2	Emporia State
79	Erik Williams	T	6-6	292	24	2	Central St., Ohio
80	Alvin Harper	WR	6-3	207	25	2	Tennessee
82	Jimmy Smith	WR	6-1	205	23	R	Jackson State
83	Kelvin Martin	WR	5-9	165	27	6	Boston College
84	Jay Novacek	TE	6-4	231	30	8	Wyoming
88	Michael Irvin	WR	6-2	199	26	5	Miami, Fla.
89	Derek Tennell	TE	6-5	270	28	5	UCLA
92	Tony Tolbert	DE	6-6	265	25	4	UT-El Paso
94	Charles Haley	DE	6-5	245	29	7	James Madison
95	Chad Hennings	DL	6-6	267	27	R	Air Force
97	Jimmie Jones	DL	6-4	276	27	3	Miami, Fla.
98	Godfrey Myles	LB	6-1	242	24	2	Florida

Injured reserve: Tony Hill, Bill Bates, Melvin Evans, Alfredo Roberts. **Reserve/physically unable to perform:** Greg Briggs, Tim Daniel, Melvin Foster, Todd Jones. **Practice squad:** Michael Beasley, Milton Biggins, Patt Evans, Jason Garrett, Fallon Wacasey (injured), Tyrone Williams.

JAY NOVACEK

ALL-PRO TIGHT END

MICHAEL IRVIN

ALL-PRO RECEIVER

Coaching staff

Head coach: Jimmy Johnson. **Assistant coaches:** Dave Wannstedt (assistant head coach/defensive coordinator/linebackers), Norv Turner (offensive coordinator/quarterbacks), Hubbard Alexander (receivers), Joe Avezzano (special teams), Joe Brodsky (running backs), Dave Campo (defensive backs), Butch Davis (defensive line), Robert Ford (tight ends), Steve Hoffman (kickers/quality control), Bob Slowik (defensive assistant), Tony Wise (offensive line), Mike Woicik (strength and conditioning).

Paul Moseley